SOCIAL SECURITY BENEFITS FOR SPOUSES AND SURVIVORS

ELEMENTS, CONSIDERATIONS, AND ADJUSTMENTS

HEALTH CARE ISSUES, COSTS AND ACCESS

Additional books in this series can be found on Nova's website under the Series tab.

Additional e-books in this series can be found on Nova's website under the e-book tab.

SOCIAL SECURITY BENEFITS FOR SPOUSES AND SURVIVORS

ELEMENTS, CONSIDERATIONS, AND ADJUSTMENTS

JULIANA LAWRENCE
EDITOR

nova publishers

New York

NOTICE TO THE READER

The Publisher has taken reasonable care in the preparation of this book, but makes no expressed or implied warranty of any kind and assumes no responsibility for any errors or omissions. No liability is assumed for incidental or consequential damages in connection with or arising out of information contained in this book. The Publisher shall not be liable for any special, consequential, or exemplary damages resulting, in whole or in part, from the readers' use of, or reliance upon, this material. Any parts of this book based on government reports are so indicated and copyright is claimed for those parts to the extent applicable to compilations of such works.

Independent verification should be sought for any data, advice or recommendations contained in this book. In addition, no responsibility is assumed by the publisher for any injury and/or damage to persons or property arising from any methods, products, instructions, ideas or otherwise contained in this publication.

This publication is designed to provide accurate and authoritative information with regard to the subject matter covered herein. It is sold with the clear understanding that the Publisher is not engaged in rendering legal or any other professional services. If legal or any other expert assistance is required, the services of a competent person should be sought. FROM A DECLARATION OF PARTICIPANTS JOINTLY ADOPTED BY A COMMITTEE OF THE AMERICAN BAR ASSOCIATION AND A COMMITTEE OF PUBLISHERS.

Additional color graphics may be available in the e-book version of this book.

Library of Congress Cataloging-in-Publication Data

ISBN: 978-1-63321-828-4

Published by Nova Science Publishers, Inc. † New York

CONTENTS

PREFACE

This book describes the current-law structure of auxiliary benefits for spouses, divorced spouses, and surviving spouses. It also discusses some of the issues concerning the adequacy and equity of the current-law structure of auxiliary benefits, and presents some recent proposals. The book also explains how the Social Security Retirement Earnings Test (RET) works under current law. In addition, it provides benefit examples to illustrate the effect of the RET on Social Security beneficiaries who are below FRA and family members who receive benefits based on their work records. It also briefly discusses policy issues, including recent research on the effect of the RET on work effort and the decision to claim Social Security benefits.

Chapter 1 – Social Security auxiliary benefits were established in 1939 when Congress extended benefits to the dependents and survivors of workers covered by Social Security. Since 1939, Social Security auxiliary benefits have been modified by Congress numerous times to change eligibility requirements for spouses, widows, children, and others and to expand eligibility for auxiliary benefits to new groups of beneficiaries, such as divorcé(e)s, husbands, and widowers.

Auxiliary benefits are paid to the spouse, former spouse, survivor, child, or parent of a Social Security-covered worker and are equal to a specified percentage of the worker's basic monthly benefit amount (subject to a maximum family benefit amount). For example, the spouse of a retired worker may receive up to 50% of the retired worker's basic benefit and the widow(er) of a retired worker may receive up to 100% of the retired worker's basic benefit.

When auxiliary benefits were first established, most households consisted of a single earner— usually the husband—and a wife who cared for children and remained out of the paid workforce. As a result, benefits for non-working spouses were structured to be relatively generous. A woman who was never employed but is married to a man with high Social Security-covered wages may receive a Social Security spousal benefit that is higher than the retirement benefit received by a single woman, or a woman who was married less than 10 years, who worked a full career in a low-wage job.

In recent decades, this household structure has changed in part because women have entered the workforce in increasing numbers. The labor force participation rate of women with children under the age of 18 increased from 47% in 1975 to 71% in 2010. As a result, many women now qualify for Social Security benefits based on their own work records. In some cases, under the current benefit structure, a two-earner household may receive lower total Social Security benefits than a single-earner household with identical total Social Security-covered earnings. Women are, however, more likely than men to take breaks in employment to care for family members, which can result in fewer years of contributions to Social Security and employer-sponsored pension plans.

Another change since 1939 has been an increase in the number of men and women who remain single or who have divorced. Persons who have never married, or who were married for less than 10 years, do not qualify for Social Security spousal or survivor benefits under current law.

Proposals to modify the Social Security auxiliary benefit structure are generally motivated by desire to improve equity for families, or adequacy for certain beneficiaries, rather than by the financial status of the Social Security system. For example, some proposals address the adequacy of benefits for certain groups of beneficiaries such as elderly and widowed women. Although Social Security plays an important role in the retirement security of aged women, about 18% of divorced women beneficiaries and 16% of never-married women beneficiaries have total incomes below the official poverty line.

This report describes the current-law structure of auxiliary benefits for spouses, divorced spouses, and surviving spouses. It also discusses some of the issues concerning the adequacy and equity of the current-law structure of auxiliary benefits, and presents some recent proposals.

Chapter 2 – Under the Social Security Retirement Earnings Test (RET), the monthly benefit of a Social Security beneficiary who is below full retirement age (FRA) is reduced if he or she has earnings that exceed an annual threshold. In 2012, a beneficiary who is below FRA and will not attain FRA during the year is subject to a $1 reduction in benefits for each $2 of earnings above $14,640. A beneficiary who will attain FRA in 2012 is subject to a $1 reduction in benefits for each $3 of earnings above $38,880. The annual exempt amounts ($14,640 and $38,880 in 2012) generally are adjusted each year according to average wage growth.

If a beneficiary is affected by the RET, his or her monthly benefit may be reduced in part or in full, depending on the total applicable reduction. For example, if the total applicable reduction is greater than the beneficiary's monthly benefit amount, no monthly benefit is payable for one or more months. If family members also receive auxiliary benefits based on the beneficiary's work record, the reduction is pro-rated and applied to all benefits payable on that work record (including benefits paid to spouses who are *above* FRA). For example, in the case of a family consisting of a worker beneficiary who has earnings above the annual exempt amount and a spouse and child who receive benefits based on his or her work record, the benefit reduction that applies under the RET is charged against the total family benefit.

The RET has been part of the Social Security program in some form throughout the program's history. The original rationale for the RET was that, as a social insurance system, Social Security protects workers from certain risks, including the loss of earnings due to retirement. Therefore, benefits should be withheld from workers who show by their earnings that they have not "retired." The RET does not apply to Social Security disability beneficiaries who are subject to separate limitations on earnings.

If a beneficiary is affected by the RET, his or her monthly benefit is *recomputed,* and the dollar amount of the monthly benefit is *increased,* when he or she attains FRA. This feature of the RET, which allows beneficiaries to recoup benefits "lost" as a result of the RET, is not widely known or understood. The benefit recomputation at FRA is done by adjusting (lessening) the actuarial reduction for retirement before FRA that was applied in the initial benefit computation to take into account months for which benefits were reduced in part or in full under the RET. Any spousal benefits that were reduced because of the RET are recomputed when the spouse attains FRA. For a spouse who has already attained FRA, however, there is no subsequent adjustment to benefits to take into account months for which no benefit or a partial benefit was paid as a result of the RET.

The Social Security Administration estimates that elimination of the RET for individuals aged 62 or older would have a negative effect on the Social Security trust fund in the amount of $81 billion from 2012 to 2018, although it would have no major effect on Social Security's projected long-range financial outlook.

This report explains how the RET works under current law. In addition, it provides benefit examples to illustrate the effect of the RET on Social Security beneficiaries who are below FRA and family members who receive benefits based on their work records. It also briefly discusses policy issues, including recent research on the effect of the RET on work effort and the decision to claim Social Security benefits.

Chapter 3 – The windfall elimination provision (WEP) reduces the Social Security benefits of workers who also have pension benefits from employment not covered by Social Security. Its purpose is to remove an advantage or "windfall" these workers would otherwise receive as a result of the interaction between the Social Security benefit formula and the workers' relatively short careers in Social Security-covered employment. Opponents contend the provision is basically imprecise and can be unfair.

Chapter 4 – Social Security spousal benefits were established in the 1930s to help support wives who are financially dependent on their husbands. It has since become more common for both spouses in a couple to work, with the result that, in more cases, both members of a couple are entitled to Social Security or other government pensions based on their own work records. Social Security does not provide both a full retired-worker and a full spousal benefit to the same individual.

Two provisions are designed to reduce the Social Security spousal benefits of individuals who are not financially dependent on their spouses because they receive benefits based on their own work records. These are

- the "dual entitlement" rule, which applies to spouses who qualify for both (1) Social Security spousal benefits based on their spouses' work histories in Social Security-covered employment and (2) their own Social Security retired- or disabled-worker benefits, based on their own work histories in Social Security-covered employment; and
- the Government Pension Offset (GPO), which applies to spouses who qualify for both (1) Social Security spousal benefits based on their spouses' work histories in Social Security-covered employment and (2) their own government pensions, based on their own work in government employment that was not covered by Social Security.

The GPO reduces Social Security spousal or widow(er)'s benefits by two-thirds of the pension from non-covered government employment. The GPO does not reduce the benefits of the spouse who was covered by Social Security.

Opponents contend that the GPO is imprecise and can be unfair. Defenders argue it is the best method currently available for preserving the spousal benefit's original intent of supporting financially dependent spouses and also for eliminating an unfair advantage for spouses working in non-Social Security-covered employment compared with spouses working in Social Security-covered jobs (who are subject to the dual entitlement rule).

In: Social Security Benefits
Editor: Juliana Lawrence

ISBN: 978-1-63321-828-4
© 2014 Nova Science Publishers, Inc.

Chapter 1

SOCIAL SECURITY: REVISITING BENEFITS FOR SPOUSES AND SURVIVORS[*]

Alison M. Shelton and Dawn Nuschler

SUMMARY

Social Security auxiliary benefits were established in 1939 when Congress extended benefits to the dependents and survivors of workers covered by Social Security. Since 1939, Social Security auxiliary benefits have been modified by Congress numerous times to change eligibility requirements for spouses, widows, children, and others and to expand eligibility for auxiliary benefits to new groups of beneficiaries, such as divorcé(e)s, husbands, and widowers.

Auxiliary benefits are paid to the spouse, former spouse, survivor, child, or parent of a Social Security-covered worker and are equal to a specified percentage of the worker's basic monthly benefit amount (subject to a maximum family benefit amount). For example, the spouse of a retired worker may receive up to 50% of the retired worker's basic benefit and the widow(er) of a retired worker may receive up to 100% of the retired worker's basic benefit.

When auxiliary benefits were first established, most households consisted of a single earner— usually the husband—and a wife who cared for children and remained out of the paid workforce. As a result, benefits

---

[*] This is an edited, reformatted and augmented version of a Congressional Research Service publication R41479, prepared for Members and Committees of Congress dated January 10, 2012.

for non-working spouses were structured to be relatively generous. A woman who was never employed but is married to a man with high Social Security-covered wages may receive a Social Security spousal benefit that is higher than the retirement benefit received by a single woman, or a woman who was married less than 10 years, who worked a full career in a low-wage job.

In recent decades, this household structure has changed in part because women have entered the workforce in increasing numbers. The labor force participation rate of women with children under the age of 18 increased from 47% in 1975 to 71% in 2010. As a result, many women now qualify for Social Security benefits based on their own work records. In some cases, under the current benefit structure, a two-earner household may receive lower total Social Security benefits than a single-earner household with identical total Social Security-covered earnings. Women are, however, more likely than men to take breaks in employment to care for family members, which can result in fewer years of contributions to Social Security and employer-sponsored pension plans.

Another change since 1939 has been an increase in the number of men and women who remain single or who have divorced. Persons who have never married, or who were married for less than 10 years, do not qualify for Social Security spousal or survivor benefits under current law.

Proposals to modify the Social Security auxiliary benefit structure are generally motivated by desire to improve equity for families, or adequacy for certain beneficiaries, rather than by the financial status of the Social Security system. For example, some proposals address the adequacy of benefits for certain groups of beneficiaries such as elderly and widowed women. Although Social Security plays an important role in the retirement security of aged women, about 18% of divorced women beneficiaries and 16% of never-married women beneficiaries have total incomes below the official poverty line.

This report describes the current-law structure of auxiliary benefits for spouses, divorced spouses, and surviving spouses. It also discusses some of the issues concerning the adequacy and equity of the current-law structure of auxiliary benefits, and presents some recent proposals.

INTRODUCTION

Social Security provides benefits, sometimes called "auxiliary benefits" or "dependents' benefits," to the spouses, former spouses, widow(er)s, children, and parents of retired, disabled, and deceased workers. Auxiliary benefits are based on the work record of the household's primary earner.

Social Security spousal benefits (i.e., benefits for a wife or husband of the primary earner) are payable to the spouse or divorced spouse of a retired or disabled worker. Social Security survivor benefits are payable to the survivors of a deceased worker as a widow(er), as a child, as a mother or father of the deceased worker's child(ren), or as a parent of the deceased worker. Although Social Security is often viewed as a program that primarily provides benefits to retired and disabled workers, 36% of new benefit awards in 2010 were made to the dependents and survivors of retired, disabled, and deceased workers.[1]

Spousal and survivor benefits play an important role in ensuring women's retirement security. About 21.0 million women aged 65 and older receive Social Security benefits, including 9.3 million women who receive retired-worker benefits, 2.0 million women who are entitled solely as the spouse of a retired worker, 3.6 million women who are entitled solely as the survivor of a deceased worker, and 6.2 million women who are dually entitled to a retired-worker benefit and a spouse or survivor benefit (for more information on dually entitled beneficiaries, see "Dually Entitled Beneficiaries" below).[2] For almost 60% of elderly women in beneficiary families, Social Security provided 50% or more of family income in 2008. For about 29% of elderly women in beneficiary families, Social Security provided 90% or more of family income in 2008.[3]

Women, however, continue to be vulnerable to poverty in old age for several reasons.

- Women are more likely to take employment breaks to care for children or parents. During 2008, 91% of men and 76% of women aged 25-54 participated in the labor force.[4] Breaks in employment result in fewer years of contributions to Social Security and employer-sponsored pension plans.

- The median earnings of women who are full-time wage and salary workers are 81% of their male counterparts.[5] Because Social Security and pension benefits are linked to earnings, this "earnings gap" can lead to lower benefit amounts for women than for men.

- Women on average live longer than men. Women reaching the age of 65 in 2012 are likely to live another 20.0 years, on average, compared with another 17.8 years for men.[6] As a consequence, women spend longer in retirement and are more vulnerable to inflation and the risk of outliving other assets. The real value of pension benefits declines with age as pensions generally are not adjusted for inflation, and some pensions cease with the death of the retired worker.

- About 9% of women aged 50-59, and about 6% of women aged 60-69, have never married and therefore do not qualify for Social Security spousal or survivor benefits.[7]

- About 5% of women aged 50-59, about 14% of women aged 60-69, and about 48% of women aged 70 and older are currently widowed. By comparison, about 2% of men aged 50-59, about 4% of men aged 60-69, and about 17% of men aged 70 and older are widowed.[8]

Spousal and survivor benefits were added to the Social Security system in 1939. At that time, the majority of households consisted of a single earner—generally the husband—and a wife who was not in the paid workforce but instead stayed home to care for children. In recent decades, women have increasingly assumed roles as equal or primary wage earners or as heads of families.

Another development over recent decades has been that increasing numbers of men and women remain single or are divorced. Social Security spousal and aged survivor benefits are not available to persons who have never married. Some argue that the unavailability of spousal and survivor benefits for women who have never been married, or who were married for less than 10 years, may be particularly problematic for minority and poor women.[9]

The current benefit structure can result in situations where a two-earner household receives lower combined Social Security benefits than a single-earner household with identical total Social Security-covered earnings. Moreover, after the death of one spouse, the disparity in benefits may increase: in a one-earner couple, the surviving spouse receives two-thirds of what the couple received on a combined basis, while in some two-earner couples with roughly equal earnings, the surviving spouse receives roughly one-half of what the couple received on a combined basis.

This report presents the current-law structure of auxiliary benefits for spouses, divorced spouses, and surviving spouses. It discusses some issues concerning the adequacy and equity of current-law spousal and widow(er)'s benefits, as well as some of the proposed changes.

ORIGINS OF SOCIAL SECURITY AUXILIARY BENEFITS

The original Social Security Act of 1935[10] established a system of Old-Age Insurance to provide benefits to individuals who were aged 65 or older and who had "earned" retirement benefits through work in jobs covered by the system. Before the Old-Age Insurance program was in full operation, the Social Security Amendments of 1939[11] extended monthly benefits to workers' dependents and survivors. The program now provided Old-Age and Survivors Insurance (OASI).[12]

The 1939 amendments established benefits for the following dependents and survivors: (1) a wife aged 65 or older; (2) a child under the age of 18; (3) a widowed mother of any age caring for an eligible child; (4) a widow aged 65 or older; and (5) a surviving dependent parent aged 65 or older.

The 1938 Social Security Advisory Council, in its report to the Social Security Board and the Senate Finance Committee, justified creating spousal benefits on the grounds of the adequacy of household benefits:

> The inadequacy of the benefits payable during the early years of the old-age insurance program is more marked where the benefits must support not only the annuitant himself but also his wife. In 1930, 63.8 per cent of men aged 65 and over were married. Payment of supplementary allowances to annuitants who have wives over 65 will increase the average benefit in such a manner as to meet the greatest social need with the minimum increase in cost. The Council believes that an additional 50 percent of the basic annuity would constitute a reasonable provision for the support of the annuitant's wife.[13]

The Social Security Board concurred in its own report, which it wrote based on the Council's report. The Board also found that benefit adequacy was the primary justification for spousal benefits:

> The Board suggests that a supplementary benefit be paid for the aged dependent wife of the retired worker which would be related to his old-age benefit. Such a plan would take account of greater presumptive need of the married couple without requiring investigation of individual need.[14]

Since 1939, auxiliary benefits have been modified by Congress many times, including the expansion of benefits to husbands, widowers, and divorced spouses. The legislative history of auxiliary benefits is outlined in detail in **Appendix A**.

AUXILIARY BENEFITS ELIGIBILITY AND DETERMINATION

Auxiliary Benefits Are Based on a Primary Earner's Benefits

Auxiliary benefits for a spouse, survivor, or other dependent are based on the benefit amount received by a primary earner (an insured worker). The primary earner may receive a Social Security retirement or disability benefit. Social Security retirement benefits are based on the average of a worker's highest 35 years of earnings. A worker's basic monthly benefit amount (primary insurance amount or PIA) is computed by applying the Social Security benefit formula to the worker's career-average, wage-indexed earnings. The benefit formula replaces a higher percentage of the pre-retirement earnings of workers with low career-average earnings than for workers with high career-average earnings.

The primary earner's initial monthly benefit is equal to his or her PIA if benefits are claimed at full retirement age (FRA, currently rising from age 65 to age 67).

A worker's initial monthly benefit will be *less* than his or her PIA if the worker begins receiving benefits *before* FRA, and it will be *greater* than his or her PIA if the worker begins receiving benefits *after* FRA. The purpose of the actuarial adjustment to benefits claimed before or after FRA is to ensure that the worker receives roughly the same total lifetime benefits regardless of when he or she claims benefits (assuming he or she lives to average life expectancy). For a detailed explanation of the Social Security retired worker benefit computation, the actuarial adjustment to benefits claimed before or after FRA and other benefit adjustments that may apply, see **Appendix B**.

Auxiliary benefits are paid to the spouse, former spouse, survivor, child, or parent of the primary earner.[15] Auxiliary benefits are determined as a percentage of the primary earner's PIA, subject to a maximum family benefit amount. For example, the spouse of a retired or disabled worker may receive up to 50% of the worker's PIA, and the widow(er) of a deceased worker may receive up to 100% of the worker's PIA. As with benefits paid to the primary earner, auxiliary benefits are subject to adjustments based on age at entitlement and other factors. A basic description of auxiliary benefits is provided in the following sections, with more detailed information provided in **Appendix C**.

Currently Married or Separated Spouses of Retired or Disabled Workers

Social Security provides a spousal benefit that is equal to 50% of a retired or disabled worker's PIA.[16] A qualifying spouse must be at least 62 years old or have a qualifying child (a child who is under the age of 16 or who receives Social Security disability benefits) in his or her care. A qualifying spouse may be either married to or separated from the worker. An individual must have been married to the worker for at least one year before he or she applies for spousal benefits, with certain exceptions. In addition, the worker must be entitled to (generally, collecting) benefits for an eligible spouse to become entitled to benefits.[17]

If a spouse claims benefits before FRA, his or her benefits are reduced to take into account the longer expected period of benefit receipt. An individual who is entitled to a Social Security benefit based on his or her own work record and to a spousal benefit in effect receives the higher of the two benefits (see "Dually Entitled Beneficiaries" below).

Widows and Widowers' Survivor Benefits

Under current law, surviving spouses (including divorced surviving spouses) may be eligible for aged widow(er)'s benefits beginning at the age of 60. If the surviving spouse receives Social Security disability benefits and meets certain other conditions, survivor benefits are available beginning at the age of 50. The aged widow(er)'s basic benefit is equal to 100% of the deceased worker's PIA.

A qualifying widow(er) must have been married to the deceased worker for at least nine months[18] and must not have remarried before the age of 60 (or before age 50 if disabled). Widow(er)s who remarry after the age of 60 (or after age 50 if disabled) may become entitled to benefits based on the prior deceased spouse's work record. (Widow(er)s who are caring for children under the age of 16 or disabled may receive survivor benefits at any age and do not have to meet the length of marriage requirement—see "Mother's and Father's Benefits" below.) Survivor benefits are not available to unmarried women, although they may be available to the natural mother or father of a deceased worker's biological child.

If an aged widow(er) claims survivor benefits before FRA, his or her monthly benefit is reduced (up to a maximum of 28.5%) to take into account the longer expected period of benefit receipt. In addition, survivor benefits may be affected by the deceased worker's decision to claim benefits before FRA under the *widow(er)'s limit provision* (see **Appendix C**). As with spouses of retired or disabled workers, a surviving spouse who is entitled to a Social Security benefit based on his or her own work record and a widow(er)'s benefit receives in effect the higher of the two benefits (see "Dually Entitled Beneficiaries" below).

Mother's and Father's Benefits

Social Security provides benefits to a surviving spouse or divorced surviving spouse of any age who is caring for the deceased worker's child, when that child is either under the age of 16 or disabled. Mother's and father's benefits are equal to 75% of the deceased worker's PIA, subject to a maximum family benefit. There are no length of marriage requirements for mother's and father's benefits, whether the beneficiary was married to, separated from or divorced from the deceased worker; however, remarriage generally ends entitlement to mother's and father's benefits.

Divorcé(e)s' Spousal and Survivor Benefits

Spousal benefits are available to a divorced spouse beginning at the age of 62, if the marriage lasted at least 10 years before the divorce became final and the person claiming spousal benefits is currently unmarried.[19] A divorced spouse who is younger than 62 years old is not eligible for spousal benefits even with an entitled child in his or her care. Survivor benefits are available to a divorced surviving spouse beginning at the age of 60 (or beginning at age 50 if disabled) if the divorced surviving spouse has not remarried before the age of 60 (or before age 50 if disabled), or if the surviving divorced spouse has an entitled child in his or her care.

Divorced spouses who are entitled to benefits receive the same spousal and survivor benefits as married or separated persons. If a divorced spouse claims benefits before FRA, his or her benefits are reduced to take into account the longer expected period of benefit receipt. In addition, a divorced spouse who is entitled to a Social Security benefit based on his or her own work record and a spousal or survivor benefit receives in effect the higher of the two benefits (see "Dually Entitled Beneficiaries" below).

Table 1. Percentage Reaching 10th Marriage Anniversary, by Marriage Cohort and Sex, for First Marriages

Year of Marriage	Male	Female
1960-1964	83.4	82.8
1965-1969	80.0	79.3
1970-1974	75.0	74.5
1975-1979	73.4	72.8
1980-1984	74.3	71.1
1985-1989	75.4	74.5
1990-1994	77.3	74.5

Source: U.S. Census Bureau, *Number, Timing and Duration of Marriages and Divorces: 2009*, Washington, DC, May 2011, Table 4, http://www.census.gov/prod/2011pubs/p70-125.pdf.

Data on Duration of Marriages

A divorced person who was married to a primary earner for less than 10 years does not qualify for spousal benefits on that spouse's record (although he or she may qualify for benefits based on his or her own record or on another spouse's record).[20] First marriages that end in divorce last about 8 years, on average.[21] **Table 1** shows that first marriages occurring from 1960 to 1964 lasted longer than those occurring in subsequent decades. About 83% of women who married for the first time during the early 1960s stayed married for 10 years or longer; however, since the 1970s, about 71%-75% of women's first marriages have lasted for at least 10 years. According to the same source, about 16% of women aged 45-49 in 2009 had been married two or more times.[22]. Other data suggest that, for men and women aged 15 to 44 in 2002, the probability of a first marriage lasting 10 years or longer was 65%. The remaining one-third of first marriages ended in divorce or separation before reaching the 10th anniversary. The probability that a first marriage would remain intact for at least 10 years was 68%, 51%, and 64% for Hispanic, black, and white women, respectively. Among women aged 45 to 49 in 2009, 16% had been married two or more times.[23]

Dually Entitled Beneficiaries

A person may qualify for a spousal or survivor benefit as well as for a Social Security benefit based on his or her own work record (a retired-worker benefit). In such cases, the person in effect receives the *higher* of the worker benefit and the spousal/survivor benefit. When the person's retired-worker benefit is higher than the spousal/survivor benefit to which he or she would be entitled, the person receives only the retired-worker benefit. Conversely, when the person's retired-worker benefit is lower than the spousal/survivor benefit, the person is referred to as "dually entitled" and receives the retired-worker benefit plus a spousal/survivor benefit that is equal to the difference between the retired-worker benefit and the full spousal/survivor benefit. In essence, the person receives a total benefit amount equal to the higher spousal benefit.

Women have increasingly become entitled to Social Security benefits based on their own work records, either as retired-worker beneficiaries only or as dually entitled beneficiaries.

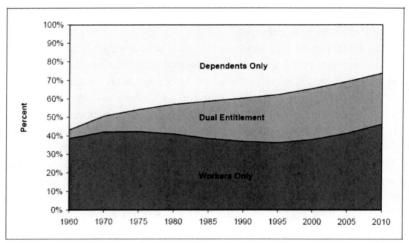

Source: U.S. Social Security Administration, *Annual Statistical Supplement, 2011*, Washington, DC, table 5.A14, http://www.ssa.gov/policy/docs/statcomps/ supplement/2011/5a.html#table5.A14.

Figure 1. Basis of Entitlement for Women Aged 62 or Older, 1960-2010, Selected Years.

As shown in **Figure 1**, the percentage of women aged 62 or older entitled to benefits based on their own work records—as retired workers or as dually entitled beneficiaries—grew from 43% in 1960 to 74% in 2010. Most of this growth was in the percentage of dually entitled beneficiaries, however. The percentage of women aged 62 or older entitled to benefits based solely on their own work records fluctuated in a range between 39% and 41% between 1960 and 2005, although this figure grew to 46% in 2010. In 2010, 54% of women aged 62 or older relied to some extent on benefits received as a spouse or survivor: about half (28%) of spouse and survivor beneficiaries were dually entitled, whereas the other half (26%) received spouse or survivor benefits only.

As shown in **Table 2**, among wives who are dually entitled spousal beneficiaries in December 2010, the retired-worker benefit accounted for 68% of the combined monthly benefit (the retired-worker benefit with a top-up provided by the spousal benefit) and the spousal benefit accounted for 32% of the combined monthly benefit, on average. Among widows who are dually entitled survivor beneficiaries, the retired-worker benefit and the widow(er)'s benefit each accounted for about half of the combined monthly benefit, on average.[24]

Table 2. Average Benefit Levels among Retired Workers with Dual Entitlement, December 2010

Type of Secondary Benefit	Number	Average Monthly Benefit:		
		Combined Benefit	Retired-Worker Benefit	Reduced Secondary Benefit
Spouses	**2,918,282**	**$723**	**$491**	**$232**
Wives of Retired & Disabled Workers	2,874,713	$724	$491	$233
Husbands of Retired & Disabled Workers	43,569	$668	$496	$172
Widow(er)s	**3,760,813**	**$1,309**	**$664**	**$646**
Widows	3,649,546	$1,311	$655	$656
Widowers	111,267	$1,242	$930	$313

Source: U.S. Social Security Administration, *Annual Statistical Supplement, 2011*, Washington, DC, table 5.G3, http://www.socialsecurity.gov/policy/docs/statcomps/supplement/2011/5g.html#table5.g3.

Many more women than men are dually entitled to retired-worker benefits and spousal or widow(er)'s benefits. As shown in the table, in December 2010, about 6.5 million women and 155,000 men were dually entitled to benefits.[25]

LABOR FORCE PARTICIPATION OF WOMEN

In 1970, about 43% of women aged 16 or older participated in the labor force, compared with about 80% of men aged 16 or older. By 2010, about 59% of women aged 16 or older participated in the labor force, compared with 71% of men in the same age group.[26] The increase in labor force participation among women since 1970 has led to an increase in the number of women who qualify for Social Security benefits based on their own work records.

Labor Force Participation of Women with Children

Women with children under the age of 18 have increasingly entered the labor force in recent decades, as shown in **Figure 2**. The labor force participation rate of women with children under the age of 18 increased from 47% in 1975 to a peak of 73% in 2000. By 2004, the rate had receded to 71% and has remained at around that level through 2010. The labor force participation rate of women with children aged 6 to 17 (none younger) rose 22 percentage points over this period, from 55% in 1975 to 77% in 2010. The labor force participation rate of women with children under the age of 6 increased 25 percentage points over this period, from 39% in 1975 to 64% in 2010. In general, in 2010, women with children aged 6-17 were more likely to participate in the labor force (77%) than women with children under the age of 6 (64%) or under the age of 3 (61%). In addition, single mothers (mothers who are never-married, divorced, separated, or widowed) are more likely to participate in the labor force (75%) than married mothers in which the spouse is present (70%).[27]

Women with children have fewer years of paid work, on average. By the age of 50, women without children who were born between 1948 and 1958 had worked on average about two years less than men overall (i.e., men with and without children). For a woman with two children, however, the gap at the age of 50 was about 6.5 years less than the average man with or without children. By the age of 50, African American women (with and without children) have worked, on average, about two years *more* than other women with and without children.[28]

For many women, caregiving is also likely to lead to part-time work. Women are more likely than men to work part time (i.e., less than 35 hours per week in a sole or principal job). In 2010, 26% of women in wage and salary jobs worked part time, compared to 13% of men. These proportions have changed little over time.[29]

In 2009, about 71% of mothers worked or were actively searching for work. About two-thirds of mothers who worked in 2009 were in a dual-earner family. The remaining third were the sole job-holders in their family, either because their spouses were unemployed or out of the labor force, or because these mothers were heads of household.[30]

Women with more education and women in later birth cohorts are also likely to have longer employment histories than other women.[31] In 2010, women accounted for more than half of all workers within several industry sectors: financial activities (women constituted 54.3% of employees in this sector), education and health services (74.7%), and leisure and hospitality (51.4). However, women were under-represented (relative to their share of total employment) in agriculture (24.5%), mining (13.8%), construction (8.9%), manufacturing (28.0%), and transportation and utilities (22.9%).[32]

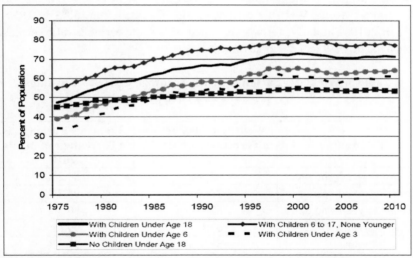

Source: Bureau of Labor Statistics, *Women in the Labor Force: A Databook*, Washington, DC, December 2011, Table 7, http://www.bls.gov/cps/wlf-databook-2011.pdf.

Figure 2. Labor Force Participation Rates of Women with Children, 1975-2010.

Earnings Gap

Another reason why women receive lower retired-worker benefits than men is that full-time women workers earn about 80%-81% of the median[33] weekly earnings of their male counterparts. In 2010, full-time women who were full-time wage and salary workers had median earnings of $669, or about 81% of the $824 median earned by their male counterparts.[34] The women's-to-men's earnings ratio was about 62% in 1979 and, after increasing gradually during the 1980s and 1990s, has been in the range of 80%-81% since 2004.

In 2010, the earnings gap between women and men varied among age groups (see **Table 3**). Among full-time workers, women aged 16-24 earned 95% as much as men; women aged 25-34 earned about 91% as much as men; and women aged 55-64 earned about 75% as much as men.

Over time, the earnings gap between women and men has narrowed for most age groups. For example, among full-time workers aged 25-34, the women's-to-men's earnings ratio increased from 68% in 1979 to 91% in 2010. For workers aged 35-44, the earnings ratio increased from 58% in 1979 to 80% in 2010. Similarly, for workers aged 45-54, the earnings ratio increased from 57% in 1979 to 77% in 2010.

Table 3. Women's Earnings as a Percentage of Men's Earnings, 1979 and 2010

Age	Women's Earnings as a Percentage of Men's, 1979	Women's Earnings as a Percentage of Men's, 2010
Total, 16 years and older	62.3%	81.2%
Total, 16 to 24 years	78.6%	95.3%
Total, 25 years and older	62.1%	80.5%
25 to 34 years	67.5%	90.8%
35 to 44 years	58.3%	79.9%
45 to 54 years	56.8%	76.5%
55 to 64 years	60.6%	75.2%
65 years and older	77.6%	75.7%

Source: Bureau of Labor Statistics, U.S. Department of Labor, *Highlights of Women's Earnings in 2010*, Washington, DC, July 2011, table 12, http://www.bls.gov/cps/cpswom2010.pdf.

Notes: Ratios are for men and women who are full-time wage and salary earners with median earnings.

Comparing the annual earnings of women and men may understate differences in total earnings across longer time periods. Using a 15-year timeframe (1983-1998), one study found that women in the prime working years of 26 to 59 had total earnings over the 15-year period that were 38% of what prime-age men earned, in total, over the same period.[35]

As women enter the work force in greater numbers, more women will qualify for Social Security benefits based on their own work records, instead of a spousal benefit that is equal to 50% of the husband's PIA. However, retired-worker and disabled-worker benefits for women continue to be lower than those for men on average for a range of reasons, as discussed above. Consequently, after the death of a husband, the survivor's benefit, which is equal to 100% of the husband's PIA, will continue to play an important role in the financial well-being of widows.

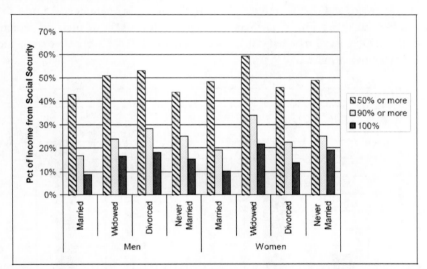

Source: Social Security Administration, *Income of the Population 55 or Older, 2008*, Washington, DC, April 2010, Table 8.B3, http://www.socialsecurity.gov/policy/docs/statcomps/income_pop55/2008/sect08.pdf.

Figure 3. Relative Importance of Social Security to Total Retirement Income for Persons Aged 65 or Older in 2008.

ADEQUACY AND EQUITY ISSUES

Adequacy Issues

Social Security is a key component of total retirement income for both men and women. **Figure 3** shows the extent to which men and women of different marital status rely on Social Security benefits. The height of the columns represents the average proportion of each subgroup that relies on Social Security for 50% or more (hatched bars), 90% or more (light bars), or 100% (dark bars) of their total retirement income.

Cutting these data a different way (not shown in **Figure 3**), among men aged 65 or older in 2008 who relied on Social Security benefits for 100% of their retirement income, 59.5% were married, 20.0% were widowed, 14.3% were divorced, and 6.2% were never married. Among women aged 65 or older in 2008 who relied on Social Security benefits for 100% of their retirement income, 27.4% were married, 58.1% were widowed, 9.5% were divorced, and 5.0% were never married.

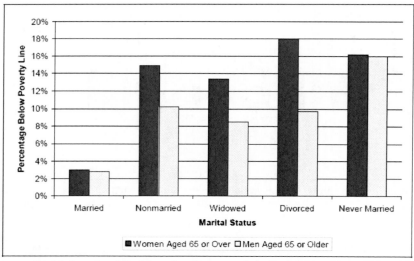

Source: Social Security Administration, *Income of the Population 55 or Older, 2008*, Washington, DC, April 2010, Table 11.3, http://www.socialsecurity.gov/policy/docs/statcomps/income_pop55/2008/sect11.pdf.

Figure 4. Poverty Status of Social Security Beneficiaries Aged 65 or Older in 2008 by Gender and Marital Status.

Social Security is credited with keeping many of the nation's elderly out of poverty. However, in 2008, 7.8% of Social Security beneficiaries aged 65 or older were below the poverty line.[36]

Figure 4 highlights the differences in poverty status among men and women aged 65 or older who receive Social Security benefits, after Social Security is combined with other sources of income such as earnings from work, pensions, income from assets, and cash public assistance. The data in the figure are for 2008. In 2008, the poverty threshold for a single person aged 65 or older was $10,326 and for a married couple with a householder aged 65 or older it was $13,030.[37]

Figure 4 shows that non-married women aged 65 or over—including widowed, divorced, and never-married women—are more likely to be in poverty than their male counterparts. Particularly vulnerable among women are divorced beneficiaries and the never-married. Among women aged 65 and over, about 18% of divorced Social Security beneficiaries and 16% of never-married Social Security beneficiaries have total incomes below the official poverty line. Research using data from the early 1990s found that divorced beneficiaries have unusually high incidence of both serious health problems and poverty.[38] Among Social Security beneficiaries aged 65 and over, poverty rates are also high among never-married men and among minority women.[39]

The poverty rate among aged widows receiving Social Security and other income fell from 41% in 1967 to 13% in 2008. By comparison, the poverty rate among widows who do not receive Social Security fell from 40% in 1967 to 33% in 2008. The drop in the poverty rate among widows who receive Social Security could be attributed in part to congressional action in 1972 to raise the benefit rate for widows to the current-law rate of 100% of the deceased worker's benefit (in 1967, 2 out of every 5 widows aged 65 or older who were receiving Social Security had income below the poverty line, but by 1973 the poverty rate among this group had fallen to just over 23%). Disabled widows remain at particular risk for poverty, however. About 39% of disabled widows who are eligible for Social Security and 59% of disabled widows who are not eligible for Social Security have total income below the poverty line.[40]

The reasons for the disparity in poverty rates among elderly men and women relate in part to women's lower lifetime earnings, which affect Social Security benefits and pensions. In addition, women live two to three years longer than men on average, making them more likely to exhaust retirement savings and other assets before death. If the deceased husband was receiving a pension, the widow's benefit may be significantly reduced, or the pension may cease with the husband's death, depending on whether the couple had a joint and survivor annuity and how the joint and survivor annuity was structured. Elderly widows also may be at risk if assets are depleted by health-related expenses prior to the death of a spouse.

Equity Issues

Although Social Security provides essential income support to non-working spouses and widows, the current-law spousal benefit structure can lead to a variety of incongruous benefit patterns that have been documented in the literature.[41] For example, a woman who was never employed but is married to a man with high Social Security-covered wages may receive a Social Security spousal benefit that is higher than the retirement benefit received by a single woman, or a woman who was married less than 10 years, who worked a full career in a low-wage job.

The current system also provides proportionately more benefits relative to payroll tax contributions to one-earner couples (which predominated when Social Security was created in the 1930s) than to single persons or to couples with two-earners, on average.

As a result, the current system can lead to situations where Social Security provides unequal benefits to one-earner and two-earner couples with the same total household earnings. Putting this in a different perspective, some two-earner couples may have to contribute significantly more to Social Security to receive the same retirement and spousal benefits that the system provides to a one-earner couple with identical total household earnings. These anomalies have become more widespread in recent decades as women's share of household income has increased, and also as women have increasingly become heads of families.

Table 4 illustrates the disparate treatment of one-earner and two-earner couples with examples developed by the American Academy of Actuaries. In the table, a one-earner couple with household earnings of $34,200 is compared with two different two-earner couples. The second couple in the comparison is a two-earner couple with the same total household earnings ($34,200) as the one-earner couple, with the earnings evenly split between the two spouses (each spouse earns $17,100). The third couple in the comparison is a two-earner couple in which one spouse earns $34,200 (the same as the primary earner in the one-earner couple) and the other spouse earns half that amount, or $17,100, for total household earnings of $51,300.

Table 4. Benefits for Three Couples with Different Earnings Splits between Husband and Wife

	First Couple: One Earner with Earnings of $34,200	Second Couple: Two Earners with Total Household Earnings of $34,200 Split Evenly	Third Couple: Two Earners with Earnings of $34,200 and $17,100
Total household earnings	$34,200	$34,200	$51,300
Spouse A earns	$34,200	$17,100	$34,200
Spouse B earns	$0	$17,100	$17,100
Annual Social Security payroll taxes(employee share only)	$2,120	$2,120	$3,180
Total monthly benefit paid to couple at retirement	$2,025 total (equals $1,350 worker benefit to Spouse A and $675 spousal benefit to Spouse B)	$1,750 total (equals $875 worker benefit to Spouse A and $875 worker benefit to Spouse B)	$2,225 total (equals $1,350 worker benefit to Spouse A and $875 worker benefit to Spouse B)
Total monthly benefit paid to survivor	$1,350	$875	$1,350

Source: American Academy of Actuaries, *Women and Social Security*, Issue Brief, June 2007.

As the table illustrates, a one-earner couple may receive higher retirement and survivor benefits than a two-earner couple with identical total household earnings. Specifically, the first couple with one earner receives a total of $2,025 in monthly retirement benefits, compared to the second couple with two earners which receives a total of $1,750 in monthly retirement benefits. Similarly, the survivor of the one-earner couple receives $1,350 in monthly benefits (either as a retired worker or as a surviving spouse). In comparison, the survivor of the two-earner couple with identical total household earnings receives $875 in monthly benefits.

In the third couple shown in **Table 4**, both spouses work in Social Security-covered employment, but in this example one spouse earns $34,200 annually and the other spouse earns $17,100. This couple receives monthly benefits that are $200 higher than the monthly benefits received by the one-earner couple ($2,225 compared with $2,025); however, this couple has earned much more over time ($17,100 annually) and contributed commensurately more in Social Security payroll taxes ($1,060 annually). The survivor benefit received by the third couple is identical to that received by the one-earner couple. Thus, the current-law Social Security spousal benefit structure requires some two-earner couples to make substantially higher contributions for similar benefit levels. With higher earnings but similar benefits to the one-earner couple, the third couple's replacement rate (i.e., initial monthly benefits as a percentage of pre-retirement earnings) is lower than that of the one-earner couple.[42]

After the death of one spouse, the disparity in benefits between one-earner and two-earner couples may increase, as shown in the table. In the one-earner couple, the surviving spouse receives a benefit equal to two-thirds of the couple's combined benefit (for a reduction equal to one-third of the couple's combined benefit).[43] In a two-earner couple with equal earnings (the second couple), the surviving spouse receives a benefit equal to one-half of the couple's combined benefit.

Further, the surviving spouse in the first couple (the one-earner couple) receives a larger monthly benefit than the survivor of the second couple (a two-earner couple with earnings evenly split)— $1,350 compared to $875— although both couples paid the same amount of Social Security payroll tax contributions. Similarly, compared to the one-earner couple, the surviving spouse in the third couple (a two-earner couple with unequal earnings and somewhat higher total earnings than the one-earner couple) receives the same monthly benefit ($1,350) although the couple paid a higher amount of Social Security payroll tax contributions. For both two-earner couples in these examples, after the death of one spouse, the second earnings record does not result in the payment of any additional benefits.[44]

In addition to inequities among couples with different work histories and earnings levels, the current structure of Social Security auxiliary benefits creates inequities among the divorced. Divorced spouses with 9½ years of marriage, for example, receive no Social Security spousal and survivor benefits, whereas divorced spouses with 10 or more years of marriage may receive full spousal and survivor benefits.

Other Considerations

The current structure of Social Security spousal and survivor benefits also raises other considerations.

- Divorced spouses receive a higher benefit after the death of their former spouse (the primary earner): benefits for a divorced spouse are equal to 50% of the primary earner's PIA, while benefits for a divorced surviving spouse are equal to 100% of the primary earner's PIA. This can create volatility in the income of divorced spouses.
- Social Security automatically provides pension rights to one or more eligible divorced spouses, in contrast to private pensions. Further, the benefit payable to the primary earner is not reduced for benefits paid to a current and/or one or more former spouses, again in contrast to private pensions.
- Widow(er)s who had high-earning spouses may face steep remarriage penalties for marrying a lower-earning second husband (if remarriage occurs before the eligibility age for widow(er)'s benefits).
- For most married women who will depend on the spousal benefit, lifetime Social Security benefits are maximized by claiming benefits as early as possible, unless the benefit based on the wife's work record is less than 40% of her husband's in which case the age differential between the two spouses becomes important in determining the wife's optimum claiming age.[45]

In response to the inequities and other issues described above, policymakers and researchers have proposed a number of ways to restructure Social Security auxiliary benefits. Some of these proposals are discussed in the following section.

PROPOSALS FOR RESTRUCTURING SOCIAL SECURITY AUXILIARY BENEFITS

A number of proposals have been put forward to modify the current structure of Social Security spousal and survivor benefits. These proposals have different potential consequences for benefit levels for current, former and surviving spouses, for the re-distribution of benefits among couples from different socio-economic levels, for what might be known as "gaming" the system to receive the maximum benefits possible, for eligibility for means-tested programs such as Supplemental Security Income and for work incentives.[46]

Earnings Sharing

Earnings sharing has been suggested as a way to address the unequal treatment of one-earner versus two-earner couples under current law. As noted above, Social Security often provides substantially higher benefits to one-earner couples than to two-earner couples with the same total household earnings. In addition, earnings sharing has sometimes been suggested as a way to provide benefits to divorced women whose marriages did not last long enough (at least 10 years) to qualify them for divorced spouse or survivor benefits. By definition, earnings sharing would not affect never-married persons.

Under the most basic form of earnings sharing, spousal and survivor benefits would be eliminated. Instead, for each year of marriage, a couple's covered earnings would be added together and divided evenly between the spouses. For years when an individual is not married, his or her own earnings would be recorded. If a person has multiple marriages, the earnings sharing would occur during each period of marriage. Both members of a couple would have individual earnings records reflecting shared earnings as a member of the couple as well as any earnings before or after the marriage. Social Security benefits would be computed separately for each member of the couple, based on the individual earnings records and using the current-law benefit formula. For couples who were married for the entire career of one or both members, both members of the couple would receive identical benefits and the couple's combined benefit would be equal to twice that of either member of the couple.

The two spouses would receive different benefits, however, if either had earnings before or after the marriage.

Earnings sharing proposals would reduce benefits for the majority of individuals, relative to current law, and in the absence of other benefit enhancements. For example, a 2009 Social Security Administration (SSA) study (hereafter, 2009 SSA Study)[47] found that 61% of individuals would receive average benefit reductions of about 17%.About 11% of individuals would experience no change in benefits, and 28% would experience benefit increases averaging about 10%.

A report issued by the House Committee on Ways and Means in 1985 examined the impact of a generic earnings sharing plan, as described above, on one-earner and two-earner couples in 2030. In the absence of transition provisions, about 64% of men and about 37% of women would have lower benefits than under current law. Average benefits for aged beneficiaries would decline by about 4.5%.[48]

Studies have found that the largest benefit reductions under earnings sharing could affect widows and divorced widows, particularly those in the lowest socioeconomic groups. The 2009 SSA study found that about 93% of widows would experience an average benefit reduction of 27% while 45% of divorced women would experience benefit reductions averaging about 22%.[49] The 1985 congressional study found that 67% of widows would experience lower benefits with the benefit loss averaging 29%, while 39% of divorced women would experience lower benefits with the benefit loss among this group averaging 31%. The decline in widow's benefits results from eliminating the surviving spouse benefit under current law and replacing it with earnings credits. The widow's benefit under current law is equal to 100% of the husband's PIA, where the husband's PIA is determined based on unshared earnings. Although earnings sharing would increase the amount of earnings credited to the surviving wife (assuming the husband was the higher earner), the benefit payable to the surviving wife based on shared earnings would be lower than the current-law widow's benefit. Another study found that, in short, the gains experienced by divorce(e)s and some married women under earnings sharing would come largely at the expense of widowed men and women.[50]

Some earnings sharing proposals would mitigate these effects by providing enhanced benefits to survivors or other targeted groups. For example, an "inheritance provision" could allow a surviving spouse to count all (instead of half) of a deceased spouse's earnings (or those of a deceased former spouse) during each year of marriage, in addition to all of his or her own earnings. An inheritance provision would protect some, though not all, surviving spouses. For example, the 2009 SSA study found that 40% of widows would receive lower benefits relative to current law under earnings sharing with an inheritance provision.

Alternatively, benefits for surviving spouses could be based on an amount equal to two-thirds of the combined benefit the couple was receiving when both members of the couple were alive (see "Survivor's Benefit Increased to 75% of Couple's Combined Benefit" below), or special provisions could be targeted to surviving disabled spouses.[51]

Provisions to protect survivors from benefit reductions, however, would reduce the amount of savings that would otherwise be achieved through program changes. Similarly, provisions to increase benefits for survivors relative to current law would increase program costs. A higher survivor benefit could be self-financed by reducing, on an actuarially fair basis, the combined benefit the couple receives while both members of the couple are alive.[52]

Divorcé(e) Benefits

Under the Social Security program, a divorced spouse must have been married to the worker for at least 10 years to qualify for spousal and survivor benefits based on the worker's record, as discussed above. Benefits for divorced spouses are equal to 50% of the worker's PIA; benefits for divorced surviving spouses are equal to 100% of the worker's PIA. One approach to extend Social Security spousal and survivor benefits to more divorced spouses would be to lower the 10-year marriage requirement (for example, to 5 or 7 years). Proposals to lower the length-of-marriage requirement for divorced spouses would improve benefit adequacy for some, although not all, divorced women.

One study estimated that lowering the marriage-duration requirement from 10 to 7 years would increase benefits for about 8% of all divorced women aged 62 or older in the year 2030. Lowering the marriage-duration requirement to 5 years would increase benefits for about 14% of all divorced women in the year 2030. The study found that, among divorced women aged 62 and over who would receive higher benefits as a result of lowering the marriage-duration requirement to 5 or 7 years, the outcomes were moderately progressive in the sense that they channeled a greater share of benefit increases to low-income and non-college-educated divorced women in old age. For example, under a 7-year marriage-duration requirement, about 13% of divorced women in the lowest retirement income quintile would receive a benefit increase compared with around 6% in the highest quintile who would receive a benefit increase. Among divorced women who gain, the average benefit in the lowest retirement income quintile would rise by 63%, compared with an average increase of 26% among divorced women in the highest quintile. However, 87% of divorced women in the lowest retirement income quintile would not receive an increase in benefits under the 7-year marriage-duration option.[53]

Some researchers contend that the 50% benefit rate for divorced spouses (50% of the worker's PIA) is not sufficient to prevent many divorcé(e)s from falling into poverty.[54] The 50% benefit rate for spouses initially was established to supplement the benefit received by a one-earner couple (i.e., in 1939, a spousal benefit was provided for a dependent wife to supplement the benefit received by the worker). Some observers contend that it may not be sufficient for persons (divorced spouses) who may be living alone. As described above, about 16.5% of divorced women and 8.7% of divorced men have incomes below the poverty line, compared to 2.3% of married men and women (see **Figure 4** above). It has been estimated that increasing the benefit rate for divorced spouses from 50% to 75% of the worker's PIA would lower the poverty rate among divorce(e)s from 30% to 11%.[55]

Increase Benefits for the Oldest Old

Another type of benefit modification would increase benefits for the oldest old (for example, beneficiaries aged 80 or older, or after 20 years of benefit receipt) by a specified percentage such as 5% or 10%. One rationale for this proposal is that beneficiaries tend to exhaust their personal savings and other assets over time, becoming more reliant on Social Security at advanced ages. Another rationale is that, after the age of 60, Social Security retirement benefits do not keep pace with rising living standards. In particular, the formula for computing a worker's initial retirement benefit is indexed to national average wage growth through the age of 60 and then to price inflation (the Consumer Price Index for Urban Wage and Clerical Workers, or CPI-W) starting at the age of 62. Once a beneficiary begins receiving benefits, his or her benefits increase each year with price inflation (the annual cost-of-living adjustment, based on the CPI-W) so that the initial benefit amount is effectively fixed in real terms. Living standards, however, tend to rise over time at a pace that exceeds price inflation.

In 2010, the National Commission on Fiscal Responsibility and Reform and the Bipartisan Policy Center both proposed packages that combined, among other measures, a benefit "bump up" after 20 years of benefit receipt, a change in the benefit formula, and a move to basing the Social Security COLA on the chained CPI-U instead of on the CPI-W.[56]

According to one study, a 5% bump-up in benefits at the age of 80[57] would result in a slight decline in poverty rates among widows and non-married retired-worker beneficiaries aged 80 or older (declines of 3% and 4%, respectively). The same study found that this option is not well-targeted toward low-income beneficiaries: less than 30% of the additional benefits would accrue to beneficiaries in the bottom quintile of the income distribution.[58]

Alternatively, a benefit increase for the oldest old could be limited to beneficiaries who receive a below-poverty-level benefit. One proposal along these lines ("longevity insurance") would provide a benefit to persons aged 82 or older that would be pro-rated based on the number of years the person contributed to Social Security.[59]

Minimum Benefit for Low Earners

Some observers argue that a carefully designed minimum benefit has the potential to reduce poverty rates among older women, including divorced and never-married women, more efficiently than existing spousal and survivor benefits.[60] Minimum benefit proposals are aimed at improving the adequacy of benefits, in comparison with some other proposals that address issues of equity among individuals and couples with different marital statuses.

Most minimum benefit proposals would require the worker to have between 20 and 30 years of Social Security-covered earnings to qualify for a minimum benefit at the poverty line or somewhat above it (for example, 120% of the poverty line).[61] These work tenure requirements are intended to address, although not resolve, concerns that providing a minimum benefit could discourage work effort. Setting eligibility for a minimum benefit at 20 to 30 years of covered earnings would allow many workers to take several years out of the labor force to care for children (or other family members) and still receive a higher benefit than they would have qualified for in the absence of a minimum benefit. Arguably, intermittent work histories play a greater role than long-term low earnings in leading to below-poverty-level benefits among women.[62] Therefore, proposals for a minimum benefit based on a specified number of years of covered employment could be combined with modified spousal benefits or with a caregiver credit to balance recognition of longer work effort with recognition of the requirements of caregiving.[63]

Some women, however, do not reach 20 years of covered earnings. About 40% of women aged 60 to 64 in 2000 had fewer than 20 years of earnings.[64] This percentage is likely to decline in younger cohorts. Moreover, minimum benefit provisions may have the unintended effect of providing minimum benefits to workers with high earnings but sporadic work histories.

To maintain the minimum benefit at a constant ratio to average living standards, some proposals would link the minimum benefit to wage growth instead of setting the minimum benefit equal to a specified percentage of the poverty line.[65] The official poverty line is indexed to price growth, whereas living standards rise with increases in wages and productivity. Wage growth generally outpaces price growth.[66]

Social Security already has a "special minimum" benefit designed to help workers with long careers at low wages.[67] The number of beneficiaries who receive the special minimum benefit under current law declines each year, however, and the Social Security Administration estimates that it is likely to cease raising benefits for new retirees in the near future.[68] A worker is awarded the special minimum benefit only if it exceeds the worker's regular benefit. The value of the special minimum benefit, which is indexed to prices, is rising more slowly than the value of the regular Social Security benefit, which is indexed to wages.

The 2010 National Commission on Fiscal Responsibility and Reform and the Bipartisan Policy Center both proposed packages that included, among other measures, provisions to create new minimum benefits.[69] Some researchers propose modernizing the special minimum benefit by tying it to a poverty level that is in line with the recommendations of the National Academy of Social Insurance.[70] If a new minimum benefit is provided, it would be necessary to address interactions between Social Security benefits and eligibility for Supplemental Security Income, Medicaid, and other means-tested programs for low-income individuals.[71]

Caregiver Credits and Drop-out Years for Caregiving

Women are more likely than men to take career breaks to care for a child or other relative, as discussed above. The Social Security retired-worker benefit is based on the average of a worker's 35 highest years of covered earnings. If a worker has fewer than 35 years of earnings, for example due to years of unpaid caregiving, years of no earnings are entered as zeros in the computation of career-average earnings. Years of zero earnings lower the worker's career-average earnings, resulting in a lower initial monthly benefit.

One approach is to replace years of low or zero earnings with a *caregiver credit* equal to a specified dollar amount. Some proposals would provide the same fixed credit to all eligible persons.[72] Other proposals would link the amount of the credit to foregone earnings, so that higher earners would receive higher credits.

The latter proposal would require that the caregiver have been in the paid labor force previously. Some proposals to base benefits on caregiving, rather than on marriage, would eliminate the current spousal benefit.[73]

A second approach is to *drop years of caregiving*, up to a fixed maximum number of years, from the benefit computation period. This approach could be implemented either by dropping years of zero earnings or by dropping years of low earnings.[74]

The proposal to drop years of zero earnings (rather than low earnings) would require a person to leave the workforce completely. This could be problematic for many women, making the proposal less likely to reach as many women as a caregiver credit. Allowing a parent to drop up to five years of zero (or low) earnings for caring for a child at home would cause the parent's AIME (average indexed monthly earnings) to be calculated based on the highest 30 years of earnings, rather than the highest 35 years of earnings (the benefit computation period would be shortened from 35 years to 30 years).

This change in the benefit computation would result in higher initial monthly benefits for these workers (and higher benefits for family members who receive benefits based on their work records).

The Social Security Disability Insurance program allows up to three "drop-out" years for caregiving.[75] Policies to credit years of caregiving in the provision of public pension benefits have been implemented in other countries in a variety of ways. In making such a provision, one question to consider is whether the credit should be available only to parents who have stopped working completely or also to parents who continue to work part-time or full-time.

Another question to consider is whether to provide credits only for the care of young children or also for the care of other immediate family members such as an aging parent.

Canada excludes years of caring for children under the age of 7 from the averaging period in the pension calculation and from the contributory period under its earnings-related scheme. Germany provides one pension point (equal to a year's contributions at the national average earnings) for three years per child, which can be taken by either the employed or non-employed parent, or shared between parents. There are also credits for working while children are under the age of 10.[76]

Other recent proposals, however, would count additional years of earnings (more than 35 years) in the Social Security benefit computation. For example, some proposals would increase the averaging period from 35 to 38 years.[77] These proposals are aimed at helping improve Social Security's projected long-range financial position and at encouraging people to work longer. Such proposals generally would affect women disproportionately.

A criticism of proposals to drop or credit years of caregiving is that they may be of most benefit to higher-wage households that can afford to forego one spouse's earnings over a period of several years. Lower-wage spouses, and single working mothers, may not be in a position to stop working for any period of time. In addition, a practical issue involves ascertaining that years out of the workforce are actually spent caring for children or other family members.

Survivor's Benefit Increased to 75% of Couple's Combined Benefit

Under current law, an aged surviving spouse receives the *higher* of his or her own retired-worker benefit and 100% of the deceased spouse's PIA. This leads to a reduction in benefits compared with the combined benefit the couple was receiving when both members of the couple were alive. The reduction ranges from one-third of the combined benefit for a one-earner couple to one-half of the combined benefit for some two-earner couples.[78] However, there is not always a corresponding reduction in household expenses for the surviving member of the couple. Some contend that 75% of the income previously shared by the couple (i.e., a reduction of 25%) more closely approximates the income needed by the surviving spouse to maintain his or her standard of living.[79]

One frequently mentioned proposal would increase the surviving spouse's benefit to the *higher* of (1) the deceased spouse's benefit, (2) the surviving spouse's own benefit, and (3) 75% of the couple's combined monthly benefit when both spouses were alive.[80] The couple's combined monthly benefit when both spouses were alive would be the sum of (1) the higher-earner's benefit and (2) the *higher* of the lower-earner's worker benefit and spousal benefit. Some proposals for a 75% survivor benefit would target the provision to lower-income households by capping the survivor benefit, for example, at the benefit amount received by the average retired-worker beneficiary.[81]

A 75% minimum survivor benefit would increase benefits for many surviving spouses, both in dollar terms and as a replacement rate for the combined benefit received by the couple when both spouses were alive. For a one-earner couple, the benefit for the surviving spouse would increase from 100% to 112% of the worker's benefit (112% = 75% of 150% of the worker's benefit that the couple received when both spouses were alive).

For a two-earner couple with similar earnings histories, the surviving spouse's benefit would increase from roughly 50% of the couple's combined benefit when both spouses were alive (under current law, the surviving spouse receives the benefit received by the higher-earning spouse while he or she was alive) to 75% of the couple's combined benefit when both spouses were alive.

A 75% minimum survivor benefit provision would "reward" the second income of a two-earner couple and improve equity between one-earner and two-earner couples. Under current law, upon the death of either spouse, the earnings record of the lower-earning spouse does not result in the payment of any additional benefits (i.e., in addition to the benefits payable on the earnings record of the higher-earning spouse). Stated another way, the earnings record of the lower-earning spouse effectively "disappears" with the death of either spouse.[82]

Because a 75% survivor benefit would increase costs to the Social Security system, some have proposed financing it through a gradual reduction in the spousal benefit from 50% to 33% of the primary earner's benefit, while both spouses are alive.[83] For a one-earner couple, the couple's combined benefit would be reduced from 150% to 133% of the worker's benefit. This is broadly consistent with the structure of private annuities, where the annuity payout is lower to adjust for a longer expected payout period. As a result, more dually entitled spouses would likely qualify for a retirement benefit based on their own work record only, because more dually entitled spouses would likely have a retired-worker benefit of their own that is equal to at least 33% (rather than 50%) of the higher-earning spouse's retired-worker benefit.[84]

Reducing a one-earner couple's combined monthly benefit to 133% of the worker's benefit, as a way to finance a 75% survivor benefit, could be problematic for low-income couples.

Effectively, the increased survivor benefit would help the survivors of both one-earner and two-earner couples, but it would be financed by reducing the combined benefits of one-earner couples from 150% to 133% of the worker's benefit.

In addition, unless this proposal were modified for divorced spouses, it would also reduce the spousal benefits received by divorce(e)s from 50% to 33% of the primary earner's benefit. After the death of the primary earner, benefits for a divorcé(e) would jump to 100% of the primary earner's benefit, creating income volatility unless this outcome is addressed for divorcé(e)s.

Although the 75% survivor benefit option could increase benefits for vulnerable groups such as aged widows, it would not address the needs of other vulnerable groups, such as individuals who were never married or who divorced before reaching 10 years of marriage.

In addition, a 75% survivor benefit option would provide somewhat more additional benefits to higher-income beneficiaries than to lower-income beneficiaries. To address this outcome, as noted above, some proposals would cap the 75% survivor benefit at the average retired-worker benefit.

CONCLUSION

This report described the current-law structure of Social Security auxiliary benefits for spouses, former spouses and surviving spouses. When Social Security auxiliary benefits were established in 1939, they were based on the typical family structure at the time consisting of a single wage-earner— generally the husband—and a wife who stayed at home to care for children and remained out of the paid workforce.

As a result, a woman who was never employed but is married to a man with high Social Security-covered wages may receive a Social Security spousal benefit that is larger than the retirement benefit received by a single woman, or a woman who was married less than 10 years, who worked a full career in a low-wage job.

In recent decades, this family structure has changed: women have entered the workforce in increasing numbers, more men and women remain single, and divorce rates have risen. As a result, more women now qualify for Social Security retirement benefits based on their own work records.

Social Security auxiliary benefits, however, continue to play a crucial role in improving income security for older women, as well as for young surviving spouses and children of deceased workers.

Women in particular continue to be vulnerable to poverty in old age and depend on the income support provided by Social Security.

Some policymakers and researchers have expressed concerns about the current structure of Social Security auxiliary benefits on both equity and adequacy grounds.

The current structure can lead to situations in which a one-earner couple receives higher retirement and survivor benefits than a two-earner couple with identical total household earnings. In addition, auxiliary benefits do not reach certain groups, such as persons who divorced before 10 years of marriage or mothers who never married.

This report presented a number of recent proposals for modifying the current structure of Social Security spousal and survivor benefits. Each of the proposals generally targets benefit increases to certain, but not all, vulnerable groups.

For example, an enhanced widow(er)'s benefit would provide income support to many elderly women and men, but it would not help those who divorced before 10 years of marriage or who never married. Similarly, a caregiver credit for workers who stay at home to care for young children would increase benefits for never-married and divorced women, but it would not help those without children, whether married or unmarried.

The consideration of potential changes to Social Security spousal and survivor benefits involves balancing improvements in benefit equity, for example, between one-earner and two-earner couples, with improvements in benefit adequacy for persons who experience relatively higher poverty rates, such as never-married men and women.

In addition, the policy discussion about auxiliary benefits may involve balancing benefit increases for spouses and survivors, divorced spouses, or never-married persons with other potential program changes to offset the higher program costs in light of the Social Security system's projected long-range financial outlook.[85]

APPENDIX A. MAJOR CHANGES IN SOCIAL SECURITY AUXILIARY BENEFITS

Amendment	Type of Benefit	Amendment	Type of Benefit
Retired Workers		**Dependents of Disabled Workers**	
1935	Retired worker aged 65 and older	1958	Same as dependents of retired-worker recipient
1956	Retired woman aged 62-64	**Survivors**	
1961	Retired man aged 62-64		*Widowed Mother*
Disabled Workers		1939	Widowed mother any age caring for eligible child
1956	Disabled worker aged 50-64		*Widow*
1960	Disabled worker under age 65	1939	Widow aged 65 and older
Dependents of Retired Workers		1956	Widow aged 62-64
	Wife	1965	Widow aged 60-61
1939	Wife aged 65 and older	1965	Divorced widow aged 60 and older
1950	Wife under age 65 caring for eligible child	1967	Disabled widow aged 50-59
1956	Wife aged 62-64		*Widower*
	Child	1950	Dependent widower aged 65 and older
1939	Child under 18	1961	Dependent widower aged 62-64
1956	Disabled child aged 18 and older	1967	Disabled dependent widower aged 50-61
1965	Full-time student aged 18-21	1972	Widower aged 60-61
1981	Student category eliminated except for high school students under age 19		*Widowed Father*

(Continued)

Amendment	Type of Benefit	Amendment	Type of Benefit
	Husband	1975[a]	Widowed father caring for eligible child
1950	Husband aged 65 and older		*Child*
1961	Husband aged 62-64	1939	Child under age 18
1978[a]	Husband under age 65 caring for eligible child	1956	Disabled child aged 18 and older
	Divorced Wife	1965	Full-time student aged 18-21
1965	Divorced wife age 62 and older	1981	Student category eliminated except for high school students under age 19
	Divorced Husband		*Parent*
1976[a]	Divorced husband aged 62 and older	1939	Dependent parent aged 65 and older
		1956	Dependent female parent aged 62-64
		1961	Dependent male parent aged 62-64

Source: CRS Report RL30565, Social Security: Summary of Major Changes in the Cash Benefits Program, May 18, 2000 (out of print).
[a] Effective date: based on court decisions, not changes in the law. In 1983, the law was changed to reflect the court decisions.

APPENDIX B. COMPUTATION OF THE SOCIAL SECURITY RETIRED-WORKER BENEFIT

To be eligible for a Social Security retired-worker benefit, a person generally needs 40 quarters of coverage, or 10 years of Social Security-covered employment (among other requirements).[86] A worker's initial monthly benefit is based on his or her 35 highest years of earnings, which are indexed to historical wage growth to bring past earnings in line with current wage levels (earnings through the age of 60 are indexed; earnings thereafter are counted at nominal value). The 35 highest years of indexed earnings are divided by 35 to determine the worker's career-average annual earnings. The resulting amount is divided by 12 to determine the worker's average indexed monthly earnings (AIME). If a worker has fewer than 35 years of earnings in covered employment (because of time out of the labor force for family caregiving, spells of unemployment or other reasons), years of no earnings are entered as zeros.

The worker's basic benefit amount (i.e., basic benefit before any adjustments for early or delayed retirement) is called the primary insurance amount (PIA). The PIA is determined by applying a formula to the AIME as shown in **Table B-1**. First, the AIME is sectioned into three brackets (or levels) of earnings. Three progressive replacement factors—90%, 32%, and 15%—are applied to the three different brackets of AIME. The three products derived from multiplying each replacement factor and bracket of AIME are added together to get the worker's PIA. Because the replacement factors are progressive, the benefit formula replaces a higher percentage of the pre-retirement earnings of workers with low career-average earnings than for workers with high career-average earnings. For workers who become eligible for retirement benefits (i.e., those who attain the age of 62), become disabled, or die in 2012, the PIA is determined as shown in the example in **Table B-1**.

Adjustment to Benefits Claimed before or after FRA

A worker's initial monthly benefit is equal to his or her PIA if he or she begins receiving benefits at FRA.[87] A worker's initial monthly benefit will be *less* than his or her PIA if he or she begins receiving benefits *before* FRA, and it will be *greater* than his or her PIA if he or she begins receiving benefits *after* FRA.

**Table B-1. Computation of a Worker's Primary Insurance Amount (PIA)
in 2012 Based on an Illustrative AIME of $5,000**

Factors	Three Brackets of AIME	PIA for Worker with an Illustrative AIME of $5,000
90%	first $767 of AIME, plus	$690.30
32%	AIME over $767 and through $4,624 plus	$1,234.20
15%	AIME over $4,624	$56.40
Total Worker's PIA (rounded down)		**$1,980.00**

Source: Congressional Research Service.

Retirement benefits are reduced by five-ninths of 1% (or 0.0056) of the worker's PIA for each month of entitlement before FRA up to 36 months, for a reduction of about 6.7% a year (from age 62 to age 65). For each month of entitlement before FRA in excess of 36 months (up to 24 months), retirement benefits are reduced by five-twelfths of 1% (or 0.0042) of the worker's PIA, for a reduction of 5% a year (from age 65 to age 67).

Workers who delay filing for benefits until after FRA receive a delayed retirement credit (DRC). The DRC applies beginning with the month the worker attains FRA and ending with the month before he or she attains the age of 70. Starting in 1990, the DRC was increased until it reached 8% per year for workers born in 1943 or later (i.e., the DRC reached 8% starting with workers who attained age 62 in 2005 or age 66 in 2009).

The actuarial adjustment to benefits claimed before or after FRA is intended to provide the worker with roughly the same total lifetime benefits regardless of the age at which he or she begins receiving benefits (assuming he or she lives to average life expectancy). Therefore, if a worker claims benefits before FRA, his or her monthly benefit is reduced to take into account the longer expected period of benefit receipt. For a worker whose FRA is 66, the decision to claim benefits at the age of 62 results in a 25% reduction in his or her PIA. For a worker whose FRA is 67, the decision to claim benefits at the age of 62 results in a 30% reduction in his or her PIA. Similarly, if a worker claims benefits after FRA, his or her monthly benefit is increased to take into account the shorter expected period of benefit receipt.

Other Adjustments to Benefits

Other benefit adjustments may apply, such as those related to simultaneous entitlement to more than one type of Social Security benefit (for more information see the section above entitled "Dually Entitled Beneficiaries"). Under the windfall elimination provision (WEP), the Social Security benefit formula is modified to reduce benefits for persons who have pensions from non-covered employment in federal, state, or local governments.[88] The Social Security maximum family benefit provision may cap total benefits received by members of a family, by reducing the benefits of individual family members.[89] Under the retirement earnings test (RET), the monthly Social Security benefit is reduced for persons who are below FRA and have wage or salary incomes above an annual dollar threshold (annual exempt amount).[90]

APPENDIX C. SUMMARY OF SOCIAL SECURITY SPOUSAL AND WIDOW(ER)'S BENEFITS UNDER CURRENT LAW

Social Security benefits for spouses and widow(er)s are based on a percentage of the worker's primary insurance amount (PIA), with various adjustments for age at entitlement and other factors. The following section describes some of the adjustments that apply to benefits for spouses and widow(er)s.

Age-Related Benefit Adjustment for Spouses

Spousal benefits (including those for divorced spouses) are reduced when the spouse claims benefits before FRA to take into account the longer expected period of benefit receipt (assuming the individual lives to average life expectancy).[91] A spouse who claims benefits at the age of 62 (the earliest eligibility age for retirement benefits) may receive a benefit that is as little as 32.5% of the worker's PIA.[92]

Age-Related Benefit Adjustments for Widow(er)s

The earliest age a widow(er) can claim benefits is age 60. If a widow or widower (including divorced and disabled widow(er)s) claims survivor benefits before FRA,[93] his or her monthly benefit is reduced up to a maximum of 28.5%[94] to take into account the longer expected period of benefit receipt (assuming he or she lives to average life expectancy).

In addition, survivor benefits may be affected by the deceased worker's decision to claim benefits before FRA. If the deceased worker claimed benefits before FRA (and therefore was receiving a reduced benefit) and the widow(er) claims survivor benefits at FRA, the widow(er)'s benefit is reduced under the *widow(er)'s limit provision*. Under the widow(er)'s limit provision, which is intended to prevent the widow(er)'s benefit from exceeding the deceased worker's retirement benefit, the widow(er)'s benefit is limited to (1) the benefit the worker would be receiving if he or she were still alive, or (2) 82.5% of the worker's PIA, whichever is higher.[95]

Benefit Adjustments Based on Other Factors

Benefits for spouses and widow(er)s may be subject to other reductions, in addition to those based on entitlement before FRA. For example, under the dual entitlement rule, a Social Security spousal or widow(er)'s benefit is reduced or fully offset if the person also receives a Social Security retired-worker or disabled-worker benefit (see "Dually Entitled Beneficiaries" above). Similarly, under the Government Pension Offset, a Social Security spousal or widow(er)'s benefit is reduced or fully offset if the person also receives a pension based on his or her own employment in certain federal, state or local government positions that are not covered by Social Security.[96] In some cases, a spousal or widow(er)'s benefit may be reduced to bring the total amount of benefits payable to family members based on the worker's record within the maximum family benefit amount (see **Appendix B**, "Other Adjustments to Benefits").[97]

Under the Social Security retirement earnings test, auxiliary benefits may be reduced if the auxiliary beneficiary is below the FRA and has earnings above specified dollar thresholds. Also, under the RET, benefits paid to spouses may be reduced if the benefits are based on the record of a worker beneficiary who is affected by the RET (excluding benefits paid to divorced spouses who have been divorced for at least two years).

Table C-1. Social Security Spousal and Widow(er)'s Benefits

Basis for Entitlement	Eligibility Age	Basic Benefit Amount Before Any Adjustments	Minimum Possible Benefit, Expressed as a Percent of the Worker's PIA[a]
Spouse	Age 62 The worker on whose record benefits are based must be receiving benefits.	50% of worker's PIA	32.5% of the worker's PIA (The figure of 32.5% is found as follows. The spousal benefit is 50% of the worker's PIA. A spouse who claims benefits at age 62 and has an FRA of 67 would have his or her spousal benefit reduced by 35%, as described in footnote 91. Mathematically, the calculation is $(1-.35)*0.50$ of the retired worker's benefit= 0.325.)
Divorced Spouse *(if divorced individual was married to the worker for at least 10 years before the divorce became final and is currently unmarried)*	Age 62 Generally, the worker on whose record benefits are based must be receiving benefits. However, a divorced spouse may receive benefits on the worker's record if the worker is eligible for (but not receiving) benefits and the divorce has been final for at least 2 years.	50% of worker's PIA	32.5% of worker's PIA (The reduction to spousal benefits for a divorced spouse who claims benefits before FRA is identical to the reduction for a married or separated spouse.)

Table C-1. (Continued)

Basis for Entitlement	Eligibility Age	Basic Benefit Amount Before Any Adjustments	Minimum Possible Benefit, Expressed as a Percent of the Worker's PIA[a]
Widowed Mothers and Fathers	No minimum age requirement	75% of deceased worker's PIA	No reduction based on age at entitlement Mother's and father's benefits end if the beneficiary becomes entitled to a widow(er)'s benefit.
Widow(er) & Divorced Widow(er) *(if divorced individual was married to the worker for at least 10 years before the divorce became final and did not remarry before age 60)*	Age 60	100% of deceased worker's PIA	71.5% of deceased worker's PIA (As described in footnote 93, the maximum reduction to the survivor benefit as a result of early entitlement is 28.5%. The figure of 71.5% is found as (1-.285) * 100% of the deceased worker's benefit. See also widow(er)'s limit provision," below.)
Disabled Widow(er) & Divorced Disabled Widow(er) *(if divorced individual was married to the worker for at least 10 years before the divorce became final and did not remarry before age 50)*	Age 50 The qualifying disability Eligibility Age must have occurred: (1) within 7 years of the worker's death; (2) within 7 years of having been previously entitled to	100% of deceased worker's PIA	71.5% of deceased worker's PIA (As described in footnote 93, the maximum reduction to the survivor benefit as a result of early entitlement is 28.5%, including for divorced survivors and disabled survivors who claim benefits before age 60.)

Basis for Entitlement	Eligibility Age	Basic Benefit Amount Before Any Adjustments	Minimum Possible Benefit, Expressed as a Percent of the Worker's PIA[a]
	benefits on the worker's record as a widow(er) with a child in his/her care; or (3) within 7 years of having been previously entitled to benefits as a disabled widow(er) that ended because the qualifying disability ended (whichever is later).[a]		
Widow(er)'s Limit Provision	As noted above, widow(er)'s benefits are reduced if a widow(er) claims benefits **before FRA**, with a maximum age-related reduction equal to 28.5% of the deceased worker's PIA. If a widow(er) claims benefits **at FRA**, his or her benefits are reduced if the deceased worker (on whose record the widow(er)'s benefit is based) claimed benefits before FRA and therefore was receiving a reduced benefit. The reduction is based on the widow(er)'s limit provision. Under this provision, the widow(er)'s benefit is limited to the *higher* of: (1) the benefit the worker would be receiving if he or she were still alive, and (2) 82.5% of the deceased worker's PIA. Stated another way, under the widow(er)'s limit provision, the maximum reduction is 17.5% of the deceased worker's PIA (i.e., no less than 82.5% of the deceased worker's PIA is payable). The widow(er)'s limit provision is intended to prevent the widow(er)'s benefit from exceeding the deceased worker's retirement benefit. Social Security Handbook, Section 724.3		

Table C-1. (Continued)

Basis for Entitlement	Eligibility Age	Basic Benefit Amount Before Any Adjustments	Minimum Possible Benefit, Expressed as a Percent of the Worker's PIA[a]
		Note Regarding the Widow(er)'s Limit Provision and the Retirement Earnings Test: If the worker died before reaching FRA and he or she had benefits fully or partially withheld for one or more months under the Social Security retirement earnings test (RET), for purposes of determining the limit on the widow(er)'s benefit, the deceased worker's benefit is recomputed and increased (at the time of his or her death) to take into account months for which benefits were withheld under the RET. (For more information, see CRS Report R41242, *Social Security Retirement Earnings Test:* *How Earnings Affect Benefits*, by Dawn Nuschler and Alison M. Shelton.)	

Source: Social Security Administration, *Social Security Handbook*, Sections 418, 420 and 724, http://www.ssa.gov/OP_Home/handbook/handbook.html.

a. The maximum reduction shown in this column reflects two steps: (1) computation of the spouse or widow(er) benefit as the applicable percentage (for example, 50% or 100%) of the retired or disabled worker's PIA,; and (2) application to the spousal or widow(er) benefit of the maximum reduction for early entitlement, assuming the spouse or widow(er) claims benefits at the earliest possible age (ages 62 and 60, respectively). For widowed mothers and fathers who have a qualified child in care, there is no reduction for entitlement before the full retirement age.

b. Benefits for disabled widow(er)s beginning at age 50 were enacted in 1967 when workers aged 50-59 needed up to seven years of covered employment to qualify for disability benefits based on their own work record.

Table C-1 shows the percentage of a worker's PIA on which various categories of spousal and widow(er)'s benefits are based. It also shows the age at which benefits are first payable on a reduced basis (the eligibility age) and the maximum reduction to benefits claimed before FRA relative to the worker's PIA.

End Notes

[1] Social Security Administration, *Fast Facts & Figures About Social Security, 2011*, Washington, DC, August 2011, p. 12, http://www.socialsecurity.gov/policy/docs/ chartbooks/fast_facts/ 2011/fast_facts11.pdf.

[2] Social Security Administration, *2011 Annual Statistical Supplement* (Washington, DC 2011), table 5.A15, http://www.socialsecurity.gov/policy/docs/statcomps/ supplement/2011/ 5a.html#table5.a15.

[3] Social Security Administration, *Income of the Aged Chartbook* (Washington, DC 2008), p. 25, http://www.socialsecurity.gov/policy/docs/chartbooks/income_aged/2008/iac08.pdf.

[4] CRS Report RL30122, *Pension Sponsorship and Participation: Summary of Recent Trends*, by John J. Topoleski, Table 1. Among workers between the ages of 25 and 64 who were employed in the private sector full-time and year-round in 2008, women were slightly more likely than men (60.1% of women compared to 58.3% of men) to work for a firm that sponsored a retirement plan, and about equally as likely as men to participate in the employer-sponsored pension plan (about 51% of both genders participated in the employer-sponsored retirement plan).

[5] Bureau of Labor Statistics, U.S. Department of Labor, *Highlights of Women's Earnings in 2010*, Washington, DC, July 2011, http://www.bls.gov/cps/cpswom2010.pdf. If the population were ranked from lowest to highest based on earnings level, the earnings level at the middle of the distribution would be the median value. At most half of the population would have earnings less than the median value, and at most half of the population would have earnings greater than the median value.

[6] Social Security Administration, The 2011 Annual Report of the Board of Trustees of the Federal Old-Age and Survivors Insurance and Federal Disability Insurance Trust Funds, Washington, DC, 2011, Table V.A3, http://www.ssa.gov/OACT/TR/2011/lr5a3.html.

[7] U.S. Census Bureau, *Number, Timing and Duration of Marriages and Divorces: 2009*, Washington, DC, May 2011, Table 6, http://www.census.gov/prod/2011pubs/p70-125.pdf.

[8] Ibid.

[9] Madonna Harrington Meyer, Douglas A. Wolf, and Christine L. Himes, *Linking Benefits to Marital Status: Race and Diminishing Access to Social Security Spouse and Widow Benefits in the U.S.*, Center for Retirement Research, Boston College, CRR WP 2004-5, Boston, MA, March 2004. See also Christopher R. Tamborini, Howard Iams, and Kevin Whitman, "Marital History, Race and Social Security: Spouse and Widow Benefit Eligibility in the United States," *Research on Aging*, vol. 31, no. 5 (2009), pp. 577-605.

[10] P.L. 271, 74th Congress. [11] P.L. 379, 76th Congress.

[12] Congress later established the Disability Insurance (DI) program in 1956.

[13] Social Security Administration, *Report of the 1938 Advisory Council on Social Security*, http://www.socialsecurity.gov/history/reports/38advise.html.

[14] Social Security Board, *A Report to the President and to the Congress of the United States*, Washington, DC, December 30, 1938, http://www.socialsecurity.gov/history/ reports/ 38ssbadvise.html.

[15] Benefits for the dependent children and parents of an insured worker are not discussed in this report.

[16] As noted above, a retired worker's own monthly benefit may be higher or lower than his or her PIA. A disabled worker's benefit is equal to his or her PIA.

[17] As discussed below, different rules may apply in the case of a divorced spouse.

[18] Exceptions are provided in some cases such as accidental death or death in the line of duty.

[19] As noted previously, generally the worker must have claimed benefits for an eligible spouse to become entitled to benefits. An eligible divorced spouse, however, may become independently entitled to benefits if the worker is eligible for (but has not yet claimed) benefits and the couple has been divorced for at least two years. (Social Security Administration, Program Operations Manual System (POMS), Section RS 00202.001 (Spouse), http://policy.ssa.gov/poms.nsf/links/0300202001) If a person has more than one former spouse, he or she is entitled to a spousal benefit based on the earnings record of the highest-earning spouse.

[20] As noted above, a divorced surviving spouse may qualify for mother's or father's benefits regardless of the length of marriage to the primary earner.

[21] U.S. Census Bureau, *Number, Timing and Duration of Marriages and Divorces: 2009*, Washington, DC, May 2011, Table 4, http://www.census.gov/prod/2011pubs/p70-125.pdf.

[22] U.S. Census Bureau, *Number, Timing and Duration of Marriages and Divorces: 2009*, Washington, DC, May 2011, page 9, http://www.census.gov/prod/2011pubs/p70-125.pdf

[23] U.S. Department of Health and Human Services, Centers for Disease Control and Prevention, National Center for Health Statistics, *Marriage and Cohabitation in the United States: A Statistical Portrait Based on Cycle 6 (2002) of the National Survey of Family Growth*, Series 23, Number 28, Washington, DC, February 2010, Figures 6 and 14 and Tables 9 and 16, available at http://www.cdc.gov/nchs/data/series/sr_23/sr23_028.pdf.

[24] U.S. Social Security Administration, *Annual Statistical Supplement, 2011*, Washington, DC, table 5.G3, http://www.socialsecurity.gov/policy/docs/statcomps/ supplement/2011/ 5g.html#table5.g3. The percentages reported here may differ slightly from the percentages represented in the table due to rounding.

[25] U.S. Social Security Administration, *Annual Statistical Supplement, 2011*, Washington, DC, table 5.G3, http://www.socialsecurity.gov/policy/docs/statcomps/ supplement/2011/ 5g.html #table5.g3.

[26] Bureau of Labor Statistics, *Women in the Labor Force: A Databook*, Washington, DC, December 2011, table 2, http://www.bls.gov/cps/wlf-databook-2011.pdf.

[27] U.S. Department of Labor, *Women in the Labor Force: A Databook*, Washington, DC, December 2011, Tables 6 and 7, http://stats.bls.gov/cps/wlf-databook-2011.pdf.

[28] Melissa M. Favreault and C. Eugene Steuerle, *The Implications of Career Lengths for Social Security*, The Urban Institute, Discussion Paper 08-03, Washington, DC, 2008, http://www.urban.org/UploadedPDF/ 411646_careerlengths.pdf.

[29] Bureau of Labor Statistics, U.S. Department of Labor, *Highlights of Women's Earnings in 2010*, Washington, DC, July 2011, page 2, http://www.bls.gov/cps/cpswom2010.pdf.

[30] U.S. Congress, Joint Economic Committee, *Understanding the Economy: Working Mothers in the Great Recession*, committee print, prepared by the Committee's majority staff, 111th Cong., May 2010, http://jec.senate.gov/public/?a= Files.Serve&File_id=c8242af9-a97b-4a97-9a9d-f7f7999911ab.

[31] Melissa M. Favreault and C. Eugene Steuerle, *The Implications of Career Lengths for Social Security*, The Urban Institute, Discussion Paper 08-03, Washington, DC, 2008, http://www.urban.org/UploadedPDF/ 411646_careerlengths.pdf.

[32] Bureau of Labor Statistics, *Women in the Labor Force: A Databook*, Washington, DC, December 2011, table 14, http://www.bls.gov/cps/wlf-databook-2011.pdf.

[33] If the population were ranked from lowest to highest based on earnings level, the earnings level at the middle of the distribution would be the median value.

[34] Bureau of Labor Statistics, U.S. Department of Labor, *Highlights of Women's Earnings in 2010*, Washington, DC, July 2011, page 1, http://www.bls.gov/cps/cpswom2010.pdf.

[35] Stephen J. Rose and Heidi I. Hartmann, *Still a Man's Labor Market: The Long-Term Earnings Gap*, Institute for Women's Policy Research, Washington, DC, 2004, http://www.iwpr.org/pdf/C355.pdf.

[36] Social Security Administration, *Income of the Population 55 or Older, 2008*, Washington, DC, April 2010, Table 11.1.

[37] U.S. Census Bureau, Poverty Thresholds 2008, http://www.census.gov/hhes/ www/poverty/ data/threshld/ thresh08.html.

[38] David A. Weaver, "The Economic Well-Being of Social Security Beneficiaries, With an Emphasis on Divorced Beneficiaries," *Social Security Bulletin*, vol. 60, no. 4 (1997).

[39] Social Security Administration, *Income of the Population 55 or Older, 2008*, Washington, DC, April 2010, Table 11.3, http://www.socialsecurity.gov/policy/docs/statcomps/ income_ pop55/2008/sect11.pdf. See also Madonna Harrington Meyer, Douglas A. Wolf, and Christine L. Himes, *Linking Benefits to Marital Status: Race and Diminishing Access to Social Security Spouse and Widow Benefits in the U.S.*, Center for Retirement Research, Boston College, CRR WP 2004-5, Boston, MA, March 2004. See also Christopher R. Tamborini, Howard Iams, and Kevin Whitman, "Marital History, Race and Social Security Spouse and Widow Benefit Eligibility in the United States," *Research on Aging*, vol. 31, no. 5 (May 2009), pp. 577-605, http://roa.sagepub.com/cgi/content/abstract/31/5/577. See also Richard W. Johnson, Melissa M. Favreault, and Joshua H. Goldwyn, *Employment, Social Security, and Future Retirement Outcomes for Single Mothers*, The Urban Institute, Washington, DC, July 2003.

[40] David A. Weaver, "Widows and Social Security," *Social Security Bulletin*, vol. 70, no. 3 (2010), pp. 89-109.

[41] See, for example, Christopher R. Tamborini and Kevin Whitman, "Women, Marriage and Social Security Benefits Revisited," *Social Security Bulletin*, vol. 67, no. 4 (2007). See also Alicia H. Munnell, Geoffrey Sanzenbacher, and Mauricio Soto, *Working Wives Reduce Social Security Replacement Rates*, Center for Retirement Research, Number 7-15, Boston, MA, October 2007.

[42] For further discussion of replacement rates among couples with different earnings histories, see Alicia H. Munnell, Geoffrey Sanzenbacher, and Mauricio Soto, *Working Wives Reduce Social Security Replacement Rates*, Center for Retirement Research, Number 7-15, Boston, MA, October 2007. The authors argue that wives' entrance into the labor market, and the ensuing rise in the ratio of wives' earnings to husbands' earnings, has lowered the replacement rate received by average-earning married couples from 50% of pre-retirement income to 45% over the past 40 years.

[43] On a combined basis, the couple received 150% of the worker's PIA. The surviving spouse receives 100% of the worker's PIA. This results in a reduction equal to one third of the couple's combined benefit.

[44] American Academy of Actuaries, *Women and Social Security*, Issue Brief, June 2007. For a related discussion, see the proposal entitled, "Survivor's Benefit Increased to 75% of Couple's Combined Benefit," below.

[45] Alicia H. Munnell and Mauricio Soto, *Why Do Women Claim Social Security Benefits So Early?*, Center for Retirement Research, Boston, MA, October 2005. The reason is that the increase in the monthly benefit from waiting to claim at the wife's FRA is generally too small to offset the reduction in total spousal benefits that is expected to occur based on men's lower-than-average life expectancy. After the husband dies, the survivor benefit is

equal to 100% of the deceased husband's PIA, regardless of when the wife first claimed benefits.

[46] For the proposals discussed in this section of the report, an estimate of the proposal's effect on the Social Security trust fund is provided when a recent estimate is available from the Social Security Administration's Office of the Chief Actuary.

[47] Howard M. Iams, Gayle L. Reznik, and Christopher R. Tamborini, "The Effects of Earnings Sharing on U.S. Social Security Benefits in 2030: An Application of the MINT Microsimulation Model," *Social Security Bulletin*, vol. 69, no. 1 (2009). SSA's study focuses on the impact of earnings sharing on benefits received by the population that will be aged 62 or older in 2030.

[48] U.S. Congress, House Committee on Ways and Means, Subcommittee on Social Security, *Report on Earnings Sharing Implementation Study*, 99th Cong., 1st sess., February 14, 1985.

[49] The 2009 SSA study also found that 96% of widowers would experience an average benefit reduction of 20%.

[50] Melissa M. Favreault and C. Eugene Steuerle, *Social Security Spouse and Survivor Benefits for the Modern Family*, The Urban Institute/The Retirement Security Project, Discussion Paper 07-01, Washington, DC, March 2007, page 19.

[51] Congressional Budget Office, *Earnings Sharing Options for the Social Security System*, Washington, DC, January 1986.

[52] Melissa M. Favreault and C. Eugene Steuerle, *Social Security Spouse and Survivor Benefits for the Modern Family*, The Urban Institute/The Retirement Security Project, Discussion Paper 07-01, Washington, DC, March 2007.

[53] Christopher R. Tamborini and Kevin Whitman, "Lowering Social Security's Duration-of-Marriage Requirement: Distributional Effects for Future Female Retirees," *Journal of Women and Aging*, vol. 22 (2010), pp. 184-203. For the purposes of the study, a "benefit increase" is defined as a 1% or greater increase in the 2030 benefit amount under the policy change, relative to current law. The study suggests that a large proportion of divorced female retirees in 2010 will have a retired-worker benefit (based on their own earnings histories) which exceeds the divorced-spouse benefit (50% of the former spouse's benefit), but which is less than the surviving divorced-spouse benefit (100% of the deceased former spouse's benefit). That is, much of the benefit increases in 2030 would accrue to divorced surviving spouses who were receiving a retired-worker benefit while the former spouse was alive but became dually-entitled upon the death of the former spouse before 2030. (Because the study addresses benefits in the year 2030, it does not include some divorced women who would receive higher benefits upon the death of a former spouse at a later date.)

[54] As discussed in David A. Weaver, "The Economic Well-Being of Social Security Beneficiaries, With an Emphasis on Divorced Beneficiaries," *Social Security Bulletin*, vol. 60, no. 4 (1997), p. 11.

[55] Ibid, p. 11.

[56] See The National Commission on Fiscal Responsibility and Reform, *The Moment of Truth*, Washington, DC, December 2010, http://www.fiscalcommission.gov/sites/fiscalcommission.gov/files/documents/TheMomentofTruth12_1_2010.pdf. See also Bipartisan Policy Center, *Restoring America's Future*, Washington, DC, November 2010, http://www.bipartisanpolicy.org/projects/debt-initiative/about.

[57] The Social Security Administration's Office of the Chief Actuary estimates that a similar proposal to provide a 5% increase to the benefit level of any beneficiary who is 85 or older at the beginning of 2011 or who reaches their 85th birthday after the beginning of 2011 would increase the Social Security trust fund's projected 75-year actuarial deficit by 4.7% of the solvency gap (based on the intermediate assumptions of the 2010 Social Security Trustees Report). The estimate is available on SSA's website http://www.ssa.gov/OACT/solvency/provisions/charts/chart_run382.html.

[58] Sharmila Choudhury, Michael V. Leonesio, and Kelvin R. Utendorf, et al., *Analysis of Social Security Proposals Intended to Help Women: Preliminary Results*, Social Security Administration, Office of Research, Evaluation, and Statistics, ORES Working Paper No. 88, Washington, DC, January 2001, p. 21.

[59] John Turner, "Longevity Insurance: Strengthening Social Security at Advanced Ages" in *Strengthening Social Security for Vulnerable Groups*, ed. National Academy of Social Insurance (Washington, DC, 2009), pp. 45-48. The full report is available at http://www.nasi.org/sites/default/files/research/ Strengthening_Social_Security_for_Vulnerable_Groups.pdf.

[60] Melissa M. Favreault, Gordon B.T. Mermin, and C. Eugene Steuerle, *Minimum Benefits in Social Security*, AARP Public Policy Institute, Washington, DC, August 2006, p. 13. See also Pamela Herd, "Ensuring a Minimum: Social Security Reform and Women," *The Gerontologist*, vol. 45, no. 1 (2005), pp. 12-25.

[61] The second model proposed by the President's Commission to Strengthen Social Security in 2001 would provide a minimum benefit set at 120% of the poverty line, payable to minimum-wage workers with 30 or more years of covered earnings. The Commission's third model would provide a minimum benefit set at 100% of the poverty line for minimum-wage workers with 30 years of covered earnings, increasing to 111% of the poverty line for minimum-wage workers with 40 years of covered earnings. See President's Commission to Strengthen Social Security, *Strengthening Social Security and Creating Personal Wealth for All Americans*, Washington, DC, December 21, 2001, http://govinfo.library.unt.edu/csss/reports/Final_report.pdfm, models 2 and 3.

[62] Melissa M. Favreault, *A New Minimum Benefit for Low Lifetime Earners*, The Urban Institute: Retirement Policy Program, Washington, DC, March 2009.

[63] Melissa M. Favreault, *A New Minimum Benefit for Low Lifetime Earners*, The Urban Institute: Retirement Policy Program, Washington, DC, March 2009.

[64] Ibid, Table 4.

[65] For example, the third model proposed by the President's Commission to Strengthen Social Security would link the minimum benefit to average wage growth. See President's Commission to Strengthen Social Security, *Strengthening Social Security and Creating Personal Wealth for All Americans*, Washington, DC, December 21, 2001, http://govinfo.library.unt.edu/csss/reports/Final_report.pdfm, model 3.

[66] While projected growth in wages over time is expected to help reduce poverty among the elderly in the future (because initial monthly Social Security benefits are indexed to average wage growth), this may be offset by benefit reductions for future beneficiaries to address Social Security's projected long-range financial imbalance.

[67] For more information on the Special Minimum Benefit, see CRS Report R41518, *Social Security: The Minimum Benefit Provision*, by Alison M. Shelton.

[68] Email from Social Security Administration staff, September 8, 2010.

[69] See The National Commission on Fiscal Responsibility and Reform, *The Moment of Truth*, Washington, DC, December 2010, http://www.fiscalcommission.gov/sites/fiscalcommission.gov/files/documents/ TheMomentofTruth12_1_2010.pdf. See also Bipartisan Policy Center, *Restoring America's Future*, Washington, DC, November 2010, http://www.bipartisanpolicy.org/projects/debt-initiative/about.

[70] Laura Sullivan, Tatjana Meschede and Thomas M. Shapiro, "Enhancing Social Security for Low-Income Workers: Coordinating an Enhanced Minimum Benefit with Social Safety Net Provisions for Seniors" in *Strengthening Social Security for Vulnerable Groups*, ed. National Academy of Social Insurance (Washington, DC, 2009), pp. 27-30. The full report is available at http://www.nasi.org/sites/default/files/research/ Strengthening_Social_Security_for_Vulnerable_Groups.pdf.

[71] The Social Security Administration's Office of the Chief Actuary provides actuarial estimates for a number of proposals that would establish a new minimum benefit or alter the current-

law special minimum benefit. Estimates are available on SSA's website at http://www.ssa.gov/OACT/solvency/provisions/benefitlevel.html (see proposals under "B5: Minimum Benefits"). For example, one proposal (item B5.1) would increase the PIA to a level such that a worker with 30 years of earnings at the minimum wage level would receive an adjusted PIA equal to 120% of the federal poverty level for an aged individual. SSA estimates that the proposal would increase the Social Security trust fund's projected 75-year actuarial deficit by 1.0% (based on the intermediate assumptions of the 2010 Social Security Trustees Report). The estimate, including more information on the proposal, is available on SSA's website at http://www.ssa.gov/OACT/solvency/provisions/charts/chart_run585.html.

[72] For example, during the 2000 presidential campaign, former Vice President Gore proposed that parents be allowed to substitute half the average wage for up to 5 years of caregiving for one child and up to 9 years of caregiving for two or more children. (To put this into perspective, in 2012, the Social Security average wage index is an estimated $45,435; half the average wage index would be about $22,718 in 2012.)

[73] The Social Security Administration's Office of the Chief Actuary provides actuarial estimates for a proposal to give parents earnings credits for up to 5 years if they have a child under the age of 6. Under the proposal, the earnings credited for a childcare year would be equal to one-half of the Social Security average wage index (or about $22,718 in 2012). SSA estimates that the proposal would increase the Social Security trust fund's projected 75-year actuarial deficit by about 14.6% (based on the intermediate assumptions of the 2010 Social Security Trustees Report). The estimate, including more information on the proposal, is available on SSA's website at http://www.ssa.gov/OACT/ solvency/provisions/charts/chart_run242.html.

[74] The 1979 Advisory Council on Social Security recommended offering drop-out years scaled to the length of service, with a maximum of 6 drop-out years (as reported in: U.S. Congress, Senate Special Committee on Aging, *Summary of Recommendations and Surveys on Social Security and Pension Policies*, committee print, 96th Cong., October 1980). The National Commission on Social Security in 1981 proposed that parents be able to credit up to 10 years of child care for children under age 6 to be counted toward qualifying for the special minimum benefit (see National Commission on Social Security, *Final Report: Social Security in America's Future*, Washington, DC, March 1981).

[75] For more information, see SSA Program Operations Manual System (POMS) §RS 00605.235 "Childcare Dropout Years," available online at http://policy.ssa.gov/poms.nsf/ lnx/ 0300605235. The childcare dropout year provision was authorized by the Social Security Disability Amendments of 1980 (P.L. 96-265) and became effective in July 1981. Between 2000 and 2011, SSA credited dropout years to 1,108 disabled beneficiaries representing about 0.15% of all SSDI beneficiaries during that period (source: CRS communication with SSA, December 2011).

[76] Organization for Economic Cooperation and Development, *Pensions at a Glance*, 2011, pp. 206 and 200.

[77] See, for example, 1994-1996 Advisory Council on Social Security, *Report vol. 1, Findings and Recommendations*, Washington, DC, January 1997, p. 19.

[78] See the discussion under "Equity Issues."

[79] American Academy of Actuaries, *Social Security Reform: Changes to the Benefit Formula and Taxation of Benefits*, Issue Brief, Washington, DC, October 2006, p. 7. See also 1994-1996 Advisory Council on Social Security, *Report vol. 1, Findings and Recommendations*, Washington, DC, January 1997, p. 19.

[80] 1994-1996 Advisory Council on Social Security, *Report vol. 1, Findings and Recommendations*, Washington, DC, January 1997, p. 19. See also Joan Entmacher, "Strengthening Social Security Benefits for Widow(er)s: The 75 Percent Combined Worker Benefit Alternative," in *Strengthening Social Security for Vulnerable Groups*, ed. National Academy of Social Insurance (Washington, DC, 2009), pp. 23-26. The full report is

available at http://www.nasi.org/ sites/default/files/research/Strengthening_ Social_ Security_for_Vulnerable_Groups.pdf.

[81] President's Commission to Strengthen Social Security, *Strengthening Social Security and Creating Personal Wealth for All Americans*, Washington, DC, December 21, 2001, http://govinfo.library.unt.edu/csss/reports/Final_report.pdfm, models 2 and 3. See also Peter A. Diamond and Peter R. Orszag, *Saving Social Security: A Balanced Approach* (Washington, DC: Brookings Institution Press, 2004), p. 105.

[82] The Social Security Administration's Office of the Chief Actuary provides actuarial estimates for a proposal to establish an alternative benefit for a surviving spouse in cases where both the husband and wife established insured status as retired workers. Under the proposal, the alternative benefit for the surviving spouse would be equal to 75% of the sum of the surviving spouse's own retired-worker benefit and the worker PIA (including any delayed retirement credits) of the deceased spouse. The alternative benefit would be payable if it is higher than the benefit payable under current law and could not exceed the benefit of a worker who is born and becomes eligible for retired-worker benefits in the same year as the surviving spouse and who earns the *SSA average wage* every year. SSA estimates that the proposal would increase the Social Security trust fund's projected 75-year actuarial deficit by 3.0% (based on the intermediate assumptions of the 2009 Social Security Trustees Report). If the alternative benefit for the surviving spouse were such that it could not exceed the benefit of a worker who is born and becomes eligible for retired-worker benefits in the same year as the surviving spouse and who earns the *taxable maximum amount* every year, the proposal would increase the Social Security trust fund's projected 75-year actuarial deficit by 15%. See Memorandum from Stephen C. Goss to Virginia Reno entitled "Estimated Financial Effects of Several Social Security Reform Options Requested by the National Academy of Social Insurance—INFORMATION," October 30, 2009, at http://www.ssa.gov/OACT/solvency/nasi_20091030.pdf (see Table 2, items D2a and D2b).

[83] Henry J. Aaron and Robert D. Reischauer, *Countdown to Reform: The Great Social Security Debate* (New York: The Century Foundation, 2001), pp. 102-106.

[84] The Social Security Administration's Office of the Chief Actuary provides actuarial estimates for a proposal to reduce the spousal benefit from 50% to 33% of the PIA of the other spouse. Under the proposal, the spousal benefit as a percentage of the other spouse's PIA would be reduced by 1 percentage point each year until it reaches 33%. SSA estimates that the proposal would reduce the Social Security trust fund's projected 75-year actuarial deficit by 6.3% (based on the intermediate assumptions of the 2010 Social Security Trustees Report). See Social Security Administration, The estimate is available on SSA's website at http://www.ssa.gov/OACT/solvency/provisions/charts/ chart_run375.html.

[85] For additional reading, see *Social Security Modernization: Options to Address Solvency and Benefit Adequacy*, Report of the Special Committee on Aging, United States Senate, S.Rept. 111-187, 111th Congress, Second Session, May 13, 2010, http://aging.senate.gov/ss/ ssreport2010.pdf.

[86] A worker needs at least 40 quarters of coverage (QCs) for a Social Security retired-worker benefit and may earn a maximum of 4 QCs per calendar year. In 2012, a worker obtains 1 QC for each $1,130 of covered earnings, up to a maximum of 4 QCs for earnings of $4,520 or more. Fewer QCs may be required for Social Security disability benefits, depending on the age at which the worker became disabled. For more information, see CRS Report RL32279, *Primer on Disability Benefits: Social Security Disability Insurance (SSDI) and Supplemental Security Income (SSI)*, by Umar Moulta-Ali.

[87] A worker may begin receiving retirement benefits as early as age 62; however, the FRA is the earliest age at which full (unreduced) retirement benefits are first payable. The FRA ranges from age 65 to age 67 depending on the worker's year of birth. The FRA is 65 for workers born before 1938; it is increasing gradually to age 67 for workers born in 1938 or later. The FRA reaches 67 for workers born in 1960 or later. The Social Security Administration

provides a chart showing the full retirement age based on year of birth, plus examples of reductions for early benefit receipt, at this link: http://www.socialsecurity.gov/retire2/agereduction.htm#chart.

[88] For more information on the windfall elimination provision, see CRS Report 98-35, *Social Security: The Windfall Elimination Provision (WEP)*, by Alison M. Shelton.

[89] The maximum family benefit varies from 150% to 188% of the retired or deceased worker's PIA (see Section 203 of the Social Security Act, 42 U.S.C. 403). The family maximum cannot be exceeded regardless of the number of beneficiaries entitled to benefits on the worker's record. If the sum of all benefits based on the worker's record exceeds the maximum family benefit, each dependent's or survivor's benefit is reduced in equal proportion to bring the total amount of benefits within the family maximum. For the family of a worker who attains age 62 or dies in 2012, the total amount of benefits payable is limited to 150% of the first $980 of PIA, plus 272% of PIA over $980 and through $1,415, plus 134% of PIA over $1,415 and through $1,845, plus; 175% of PIA over $1,845.

The dollar amounts in the benefit formula (known as "bend points") are indexed to average wage growth, as in the primary benefit formula. A different family maximum applies in the case of a disabled worker. For the family of a worker who is entitled to disability benefits, the maximum family benefit is the lesser of 85% of the worker's AIME or 150% of the worker's PIA. In no case, however, can the family benefit be less than 100% of the worker's PIA.

[90] For more information on the retirement earnings test, see CRS Report R41242, *Social Security Retirement Earnings Test: How Earnings Affect Benefits*, by Dawn Nuschler and Alison M. Shelton.

[91] Spousal benefits are reduced by 25/36 of 1% (or 0.0069) for each month of entitlement before FRA, up to 36 months, and by five-twelfths of 1% (or 0.0042) for each month of entitlement before FRA in excess of 36 months. The reduction is applied to the base spousal benefit, which is 50% of the worker's PIA. The spousal benefit is not reduced for entitlement before FRA if the spouse is caring for a qualifying child.

[92] For example, if the worker's PIA is $1,000, the spousal benefit payable at the spouse's FRA is 50% of this amount, or $500. If the spouse claims benefits at age 62 and his or her FRA is 67, the spousal benefit is reduced by 35%, from $500 to $325 per month. (The percent reduction for entitlement to benefits five years before FRA is found as the sum of (25/36) * 36 months plus (5/12) * 24 months, for a total reduction of 35%.) The spouse's benefit of $325 is equal to 32.5% of the worker's PIA of $1,000. The following link at the Social Security Administration's website allows users to see how timing the receipt of spousal benefits can affect benefit amounts: http://www.ssa.gov/OACT/quickcalc/ spouse.html.

[93] The FRA is increasing gradually from age 65 to age 67. While the FRA for retired workers and spouses will reach age 67 for persons born in 1960 or later, it will reach age 67 for widow(er)s born in 1962 or later. The Social Security Administration provides FRAs for widow(er)s based on year of birth, plus examples of reductions for early benefit receipt, available at https://www.ssa.gov/survivorchartred.htm.

[94] Survivor benefits are reduced for each month of entitlement before FRA by a fraction derived by dividing 28.5% (the maximum reduction) by the number of possible months of early retirement, which is the number of months between age 60 and the person's FRA. For example, a person whose FRA is 66 could claim benefits at age 60 and potentially receive benefits for up to 72 months before FRA. The reduction for each month before FRA is therefore 28.5% ÷ 72 = 0.00396. As a result of this methodology, the fractions involved in reducing the widow(er)'s benefit for entitlement before FRA vary depending on the date of birth and the FRA associated with that birthdate. Survivor benefits paid from ages 50 to 59 based on a disability are not further reduced. The maximum reduction of 28.5% and the procedure for finding reduction amounts for widow(er)s who retire between age 60 and

FRA are described in Social Security Administration, *Handbook*, section 724, available at http://www.socialsecurity.gov/OP_Home/handbook/handbook.07/ handbook-0724.html.

[95] For more information, see David A. Weaver, *The Widow(er)'s Limit Provision of Social Security*, Social Security Administration, Office of Policy, Office of Research, Evaluation, and Statistics, Working Paper Series Number 92, June 2001, http://www.socialsecurity.gov/policy/docs/workingpapers/wp92.pdf. If the worker died before attaining FRA and he or she had benefits withheld under the retirement earnings test (RET), for purposes of determining the limit on the widow(er)'s benefit, the worker's benefit is recomputed and *increased* at the time of the worker's death to take into account months for which the worker's benefits were partially or fully withheld under the RET. For more information on the RET and how it affects benefits for survivors, see CRS Report R41242, *Social Security Retirement Earnings Test: How Earnings Affect Benefits*, by Dawn Nuschler and Alison M. Shelton.

[96] See CRS Report RL32453, *Social Security: The Government Pension Offset (GPO)*, by Alison M. Shelton.

[97] Benefits for a divorced spouse, a surviving divorced spouse or a disabled surviving divorced spouse are not reduced for the family maximum. Benefits for other auxiliaries and survivors are reduced for the family maximum not taking into account the divorced beneficiary. Social Security Administration, Program Operations Manual System (POMS), Section RS 00615.682 (Family Benefits Where a Divorced Spouse or a Surviving Divorced Spouse is Entitled), https://secure.ssa.gov/apps10/poms.nsf/lnx/0300615682.

In: Social Security Benefits   ISBN: 978-1-63321-828-4
Editor: Juliana Lawrence   © 2014 Nova Science Publishers, Inc.

Chapter 2

SOCIAL SECURITY RETIREMENT EARNINGS TEST: HOW EARNINGS AFFECT BENEFITS[*]

Dawn Nuschler and Alison M. Shelton

SUMMARY

Under the Social Security Retirement Earnings Test (RET), the monthly benefit of a Social Security beneficiary who is below full retirement age (FRA) is reduced if he or she has earnings that exceed an annual threshold. In 2012, a beneficiary who is below FRA and will not attain FRA during the year is subject to a $1 reduction in benefits for each $2 of earnings above $14,640. A beneficiary who will attain FRA in 2012 is subject to a $1 reduction in benefits for each $3 of earnings above $38,880. The annual exempt amounts ($14,640 and $38,880 in 2012) generally are adjusted each year according to average wage growth.

If a beneficiary is affected by the RET, his or her monthly benefit may be reduced in part or in full, depending on the total applicable reduction. For example, if the total applicable reduction is greater than the beneficiary's monthly benefit amount, no monthly benefit is payable for one or more months. If family members also receive auxiliary benefits based on the beneficiary's work record, the reduction is pro-rated and applied to all benefits payable on that work record (including benefits paid to spouses who are *above* FRA). For example, in the case of a family consisting of a worker beneficiary who has earnings above the annual

---

[*] This is an edited, reformatted and augmented version of a Congressional Research Service publication, No. R41242, dated January 4, 2012.

exempt amount and a spouse and child who receive benefits based on his or her work record, the benefit reduction that applies under the RET is charged against the total family benefit.

The RET has been part of the Social Security program in some form throughout the program's history. The original rationale for the RET was that, as a social insurance system, Social Security protects workers from certain risks, including the loss of earnings due to retirement. Therefore, benefits should be withheld from workers who show by their earnings that they have not "retired." The RET does not apply to Social Security disability beneficiaries who are subject to separate limitations on earnings.

If a beneficiary is affected by the RET, his or her monthly benefit is *recomputed,* and the dollar amount of the monthly benefit is *increased,* when he or she attains FRA. This feature of the RET, which allows beneficiaries to recoup benefits "lost" as a result of the RET, is not widely known or understood. The benefit recomputation at FRA is done by adjusting (lessening) the actuarial reduction for retirement before FRA that was applied in the initial benefit computation to take into account months for which benefits were reduced in part or in full under the RET. Any spousal benefits that were reduced because of the RET are recomputed when the spouse attains FRA. For a spouse who has already attained FRA, however, there is no subsequent adjustment to benefits to take into account months for which no benefit or a partial benefit was paid as a result of the RET.

The Social Security Administration estimates that elimination of the RET for individuals aged 62 or older would have a negative effect on the Social Security trust fund in the amount of $81 billion from 2012 to 2018, although it would have no major effect on Social Security's projected long-range financial outlook.

This report explains how the RET works under current law. In addition, it provides benefit examples to illustrate the effect of the RET on Social Security beneficiaries who are below FRA and family members who receive benefits based on their work records. It also briefly discusses policy issues, including recent research on the effect of the RET on work effort and the decision to claim Social Security benefits.

INTRODUCTION

Social Security benefits received before a person attains full retirement age (FRA)[1] are subject to an actuarial reduction for early retirement and also may be reduced by the Social Security Retirement Earnings Test (RET) if the beneficiary has earnings that exceed an annual threshold. Under the RET, a beneficiary who is below FRA and will not attain FRA during the calendar year is subject to a $1 reduction in benefits for each $2 of earnings above an annual exempt amount, which is $14,640 in 2012. During the calendar year in which a beneficiary attains FRA, he or she is subject to a $1 reduction in benefits for each $3 of earnings above a higher annual exempt amount, which is $38,880 in 2012.[2]

This report explains how the RET is applied under current law and provides detailed benefit examples to show how the RET affects both the worker beneficiary and any family members (auxiliary beneficiaries) who receive benefits based on the worker beneficiary's record. The report points out features of the RET that are not widely known or understood, such as the recomputation of benefits when a beneficiary attains FRA to adjust (increase) benefits to take into account months for which no benefit or a partial benefit was paid as a result of the RET. Finally, the report discusses policy issues related to the RET, including recent research on the effect of the RET on work effort and the decision to claim Social Security benefits.

Key points discussed in the report include the following:

- Benefits may be reduced in part or in full for one or more months as a result of the RET.
- Benefit reductions under the RET apply both to the worker beneficiary and to any family members (auxiliary beneficiaries) who receive benefits based on the worker beneficiary's record. This would include, for example, a dependent child and a spouse who may have already attained FRA.
- When a worker beneficiary and family members are subject to a benefit reduction under the RET, the reduction is pro-rated and applied to each person's benefit in proportion to each person's original entitlement amount. (The total amount of the reduction remains the same, but the reduction is pro-rated across more people.)
- An auxiliary beneficiary may be subject to a reduction in benefits under the RET both on the basis of the worker beneficiary's earnings above the exempt amount and on the basis of his or her own earnings above the exempt amount.
- Benefits "lost" as a result of the RET may be recouped by the beneficiary. When a beneficiary attains FRA and is no longer subject to the RET, his or her benefits are adjusted upward to take into account months for which no benefit or a partial benefit was paid as a result of the RET.

- The Social Security Administration (SSA) estimates that elimination of the RET for individuals aged 62 or older would have no major effect on Social Security's projected long-range financial outlook. In the short run, however, SSA estimates that eliminating the RET would have a negative effect on the Social Security trust fund in the amount of $81 billion from 2012 to 2018.
- The RET raises several policy issues, including the effect of the RET on labor supply (how many hours to work and when to retire) and its effect on when workers claim Social Security benefits.

HISTORICAL BACKGROUND

In general, Social Security benefits are meant to replace, in part, earnings lost to an individual or family because of retirement, disability, or death. The rationale for the RET was outlined in the 1935 report of the Committee on Economic Security, which recommended that no benefits be paid before a person had "retired from gainful employment."[3]

The original Social Security Act barred payment of benefits for any month in which a beneficiary received wages from "regular employment."[4] This provision never went into effect, however, because the Social Security Board and many other analysts thought it would be nearly impossible to determine what was "regular" employment in different industries and occupations. Instead, the board recommended a specific monetary amount to simplify administration. In 1939, Congress incorporated these recommendations in amendments to the Social Security Act.[5] Starting with the first benefits paid in 1940, benefits were withheld for months in which covered earnings were $15 or more.

The RET has evolved from a monthly test to an annual one (with the exception of the "grace year" as discussed below) and from a provision that initially affected all worker beneficiaries to one that affects beneficiaries who are below the FRA. The most recent legislative change to the RET was in 2000 when Congress eliminated the RET for beneficiaries beginning with the month they attain FRA. This change was made under the Senior Citizens Freedom to Work Act (P.L. 106-182). Before the change in 2000, the RET applied to beneficiaries until they attained the age of 70.

CURRENT LAW

Social Security Worker and Auxiliary Benefits

Social Security benefits are based on the average of a worker's highest 35 years of earnings. A worker's primary insurance amount (PIA) is computed by applying the Social Security benefit formula to the worker's career-average, wage-indexed earnings. The benefit formula replaces a higher percentage of the pre-retirement earnings of workers with low career-average earnings than for workers with high career-average earnings.

A worker's initial monthly benefit is equal to the worker's PIA if he or she begins receiving benefits at FRA. A worker's initial monthly benefit will be *less* than his or her PIA if the worker begins receiving benefits *before* FRA, and it will be *greater* than his or her PIA if the worker begins receiving benefits *after* FRA.[6] For a more detailed explanation of the Social Security benefit computation and the actuarial adjustment to benefits claimed before or after FRA, see **Appendix A**.

Social Security also provides auxiliary benefits to eligible family members of a retired, disabled or deceased worker. Benefits payable to family members are equal to a specified percentage of the worker's PIA. For example, a spouse's benefit is equal to 50% of the worker's PIA, and a widow(er)'s benefit is equal to 100% of the deceased worker's PIA. The total amount of benefits payable to a family based on a retired or deceased worker's record is capped by the maximum family benefit amount, which varies from 150% to 188% of the retired or deceased worker's PIA. For more information on auxiliary benefits and the maximum family benefit amount, see **Appendix B**.

The RET Applies to Beneficiaries Below the Social Security Full Retirement Age

The RET applies to beneficiaries who are below the Social Security FRA and have earnings that exceed a specified dollar amount (an annual exempt amount). The RET does not apply to worker beneficiaries who are at or above FRA (the RET no longer applies beginning with the month the beneficiary attains FRA) or to those who are disabled.[7] In addition, the RET does not apply to beneficiaries living outside the United States whose work is not covered by the U.S Social Security system; in this case, the "foreign work test" is applied. Self-employed persons are subject to the RET if they have performed "substantial services," which are determined by the nature of the service performed rather than by profit or loss.

The RET Reduces Social Security Benefits

For beneficiaries who are below FRA and will not attain FRA during the calendar year, Social Security benefits are reduced by $1 for each $2 earned above the exempt amount. For beneficiaries who will attain FRA during the calendar year, Social Security benefits are reduced by $1 for each $3 earned above the exempt amount.[8]

Earnings above the exempt amount are charged against monthly benefits beginning with the first chargeable month of the year, at the applicable rate of $1 for each $2 or $3 of earnings above the exempt amount, and continue to be charged each month until all earnings above the exempt amount have been charged against the worker's benefits and any benefits payable to family members on his or her work record. A partial benefit is paid when the charge to a given month is less than the monthly benefit.

The RET Exempt Amounts

The RET applies only to wage and salary income (i.e., earnings from work). It does not apply to income from pensions, rents, dividends, interest, and other types of "unearned" income.

The RET annual exempt amounts in 2012 are $14,640 for beneficiaries who are below FRA and will not attain FRA in 2012, and $38,880 for beneficiaries who will attain FRA in 2012. The RET exempt amounts generally increase each year at the same rate as average wages in the economy.[9] **Appendix C** shows the annual exempt amounts under the RET from calendar years 2000 to 2012.

Grace Year

A "grace year" applies during the first year of benefit entitlement (or, for dependent beneficiaries, in the last year of benefit entitlement). During the grace year, the RET is applied effectively on a monthly basis. A beneficiary may receive full benefits for any month during which his or her earnings do not exceed one-twelfth of the annual exempt amount, regardless of the total amount of earnings for the year.

As an example, consider a worker aged 62 who (1) has $60,000 in earnings from January through June 2012, (2) claims Social Security retirement benefits on July 1, 2012, and (3) has no additional earnings for the remainder of the year (July through December 2012). Because this person does not have earnings above the 2012 monthly exempt amount of $1,220 in any month from July through December 2012, full benefits are paid for each month of the second half of the year. This is the case even though this person's total earnings for 2012 are $60,000, an amount higher than the 2012 annual exempt amount of $14,640.

The RET May Affect Social Security Benefits Received by Spouses, Survivors and Other Dependents

There are two ways in which a person who receives Social Security auxiliary benefits (benefits paid to spouses, survivors, and other dependents) could be affected by the RET. First, benefits paid to spouses and dependents are affected by the RET when the benefits are based on the record of a worker beneficiary who is subject to the RET (i.e., the worker beneficiary is below FRA and has earnings above the exempt amount). This includes benefits paid to spouses who are below FRA as well as to those who are *above* FRA. An exception is made for auxiliary benefits paid to divorced spouses. If a divorced spouse has been divorced from the worker beneficiary for at least two years, the auxiliary benefit is not affected by the worker beneficiary's earnings.

Second, benefits paid to spouses (including divorced spouses) and dependents are affected by the RET when the auxiliary beneficiary is below FRA and has his or her own earnings above the exempt amount. Auxiliary beneficiaries are subject to the same annual exempt amounts and benefit reduction rates that apply to worker beneficiaries.

Dually Entitled Beneficiaries

A person receiving spousal benefits who is affected by the RET based on his or her own earnings above the exempt amount may be simultaneously (dually) entitled to a retired-worker benefit based on his or her own work record. A dually entitled beneficiary receives his or her own retired-worker benefit first, plus any spousal benefit remaining after the spousal benefit is reduced based on the retired-worker benefit. In effect, the total benefit payable to a dually entitled beneficiary is capped at the higher of the retired-worker benefit and the spousal benefit.

In the case of a dually entitled beneficiary, his or her own earnings above the exempt amount affect both his or her own retired-worker benefit and the spousal benefit.[10] In addition, if the worker beneficiary on whose record the spousal benefit is based has earnings above the exempt amount, the spousal benefit is affected by those earnings as well. When a dually entitled beneficiary attains FRA, each benefit that was affected by the RET (the retired-worker benefit or the spousal benefit) is adjusted upward to take into account months for which no benefit or a partial benefit was paid as a result of the RET.

An example is provided later in the report to show how benefits paid to a non-working spouse are affected when the worker beneficiary has earnings above the exempt amount. In addition, an example is provided to show how spousal benefits are affected when both the worker beneficiary and the spouse have earnings above the exempt amount.

BENEFITS WITHHELD UNDER THE RET ARE RESTORED STARTING AT FRA

When a beneficiary has had benefits fully or partially withheld under the RET, benefits "lost" as a result of the RET are restored starting at FRA. Specifically, the worker's benefits are recomputed—and increased—when he or she attains FRA. In the benefit recomputation at FRA, the actuarial reduction for benefit entitlement before FRA that was applied in the initial benefit computation is adjusted (the actuarial reduction for early retirement is lessened) to reflect the number of months the worker received no benefit or a partial benefit as a result of the RET.[11]

In the initial benefit computation, retirement benefits are reduced for early retirement by a fraction of the worker's PIA for each month of entitlement before FRA. Retirement benefits are reduced by five-ninths of 1% (or 0.0056) of the worker's PIA for each of the first 36 months of entitlement before FRA. Stated another way, the actuarial reduction for early retirement is about 6.7% per year for the first three years of entitlement before FRA (i.e., from the age of 62 to 65). For each additional month of entitlement before FRA (up to 24 months), retirement benefits are reduced by five-twelfths of 1% (or 0.0042) of the worker's PIA, for an actuarial reduction of 5% per year (i.e., from the age of 65 to 67).[12]

Stated generally, if a worker's benefits are reduced in the initial benefit computation to reflect *x months* of early retirement, and the worker subsequently has benefits withheld under the RET for *y months*, the benefit recomputation at FRA will reflect an actuarial reduction for *x minus y months* of early retirement, resulting in a higher monthly benefit amount starting at FRA.

As an example, consider a worker who starts receiving Social Security retirement benefits at the age of 62, although his or her FRA is 66, and he or she has earnings above the RET exempt amount. Because the person claims retirement benefits four years before attaining FRA and has earnings above the RET threshold, he or she will be subject to both the actuarial reduction for benefit entitlement before FRA and benefit withholding under the RET. The actuarial reduction is equal to about 6.7% per year for the first three years of benefit entitlement before FRA and 5% per year thereafter. In this example, the total actuarial reduction in the person's initial monthly benefit is 25% ((6.7% * 3 years) + (5% * 1 year)). In addition, the person continues to work throughout the four-year period from the age of 62 to 66 and has earnings high enough to cause a reduction in his or her monthly benefit under the RET.[13] If the RET results in a 50% reduction in Social Security benefits in each of the four years from the age of 62 to 66, the person would have benefits withheld for six months each year, for a total of 24 months.[14] The benefit recomputation when the person attains FRA will take into account that the person received no benefits for 24 months as a result of the RET. Specifically, the reduction factor for benefit entitlement before FRA will be adjusted from 48 months to 24 months. Starting at FRA, the person's monthly benefit will be increased to reflect an actuarial reduction for benefit entitlement before FRA of about 13.4% (6.7% * 2 years), instead of 25%. The person receives a higher monthly benefit because benefits withheld under the RET are restored starting at FRA.

If spousal benefits are withheld under the RET (as discussed in section "The RET May Affect Social Security Benefits Received by Spouses, Survivors and Other Dependents"), they will be adjusted upward when the spouse attains FRA (not when the worker beneficiary attains FRA). For a spouse who has already attained FRA, there is no subsequent adjustment to benefits to take into account months for which no benefit or a partial benefit was paid as a result of the RET.

WORKER BENEFICIARIES WITH EARNINGS IN 2006

Table 1 shows the number of worker beneficiaries who had earnings in 2006, the most recent year for which data are available. About 1.3 million worker beneficiaries who were below FRA during all or part of 2006 had earnings.

Table 1. Number of Worker Beneficiaries with Earnings in 2006

Earnings	Below FRA Throughout 2006[a]	Attained FRA in 2006[b]
$1 - 4,999	356,000	117,500
5,000 - 9,999	226,500	69,900
10,000 - 14,999	213,500	60,900
15,000 - 19,999	72,800	35,800
20,000 - 24,999	39,200	17,100
25,000 - 29,999	17,600	9,700
30,000 - 34,999	10,200	7,800
35,000 - 39,999	6,300	6,000
40,000 - 44,999	5,600	2,100
45,000 - 49,999	3,600	1,700
50,000 - 54,999	2,500	1,500
55,000 - 59,999	2,100	1,300
60,000 - 64,999	1,800	700
65,000 - 69,999	1,300	800
70,000 - 74,999	1,300	500
75,000 - 79,999	1,000	700
80,000 - 84,999	800	600
85,000 - 89,999	900	400
90,000 - 99,999	900	800
100,000 or more	5,400	3,100
Total with Earnings	969,300	338,900

Sources: Social Security Administration, Office of Research, Evaluation and Statistics: 2007 1 Percent Continuous Work History Sample and 2006 Employee and Employer File. Data provided by the Social Security Administration to the Congressional Research Service on February 24, 2011.

Note: Table includes individuals who were awarded retired-worker benefits by December 2005.

[a] The exempt amounts for persons who were below FRA throughout 2006 were $12,480 annually and $1,040 monthly.

[b] The exempt amounts for persons who attained FRA in 2006 were $33,240 annually and $2,770 monthly.

With respect to the data shown in Table 1, it is important to note that not all worker beneficiaries with earnings are affected by the RET. For example, those who have earnings below the exempt amount are not affected by the RET. In addition, those who are in the first year of entitlement may benefit from the "grace year" provision and are not subject to the RET during any months in which they have earnings that are lower than the monthly RET exempt amount (i.e., the annual RET exempt amount divided by 12).

APPLICATION OF THE RETIREMENT EARNINGS TEST

Table 2 illustrates the application of the RET to a single person who receives benefits based on his or her own work record. The table illustrates the effect of the RET on single worker beneficiaries in two different age groups, reflecting the application of different annual exempt amounts and benefit reduction rates under the RET for beneficiaries who will remain below FRA throughout the calendar year and beneficiaries who will attain FRA during the calendar year.

The two single worker beneficiaries in the examples have the following characteristics:

Single Worker Beneficiary Who is Below FRA Throughout the Calendar Year. This example shows a worker beneficiary with a monthly benefit amount of $2,000 (this amount has already been adjusted for retirement before FRA) and $40,000 of earnings in 2012. Because this worker beneficiary is below FRA throughout the calendar year, he or she is subject to a $1 reduction in benefits for each $2 of earnings above the annual exempt amount of $14,640 in 2012.

Single Worker Beneficiary Who Will Attain FRA During the Calendar Year. This example shows a worker beneficiary with a monthly benefit amount of $2,000 (this amount has already been adjusted for retirement before FRA) and $40,000 of earnings in 2012. Because this worker beneficiary will attain FRA during the calendar year, he or she is subject to a $1 reduction in benefits for each $3 of earnings above the annual exempt amount of $38,880 in 2012.

Table 2. Application of the Retirement Earnings Test to a Single Worker Beneficiary with Earnings Above the Annual Exempt Amount, 2012

Step	Worker Beneficiary is Below FRA Throughout Calendar Year	Worker Beneficiary Will Attain FRA During Calendar Year
1. Social Security monthly benefit	$2,000	$2,000
2. Calculation of earnings above annual exempt amount		
Earnings in 2012	$40,000	$40,000
RET exempt amount in 2012	$14,640	$38,880
Earnings above annual exempt amount	$25,360	$1,120
3. RET charge (= one-half of earnings above exempt amount for beneficiary below FRA, or one-third of earnings above exempt amount for beneficiary who will attain FRA during calendar year)	$12,680	$560
4. Application of the RET. The benefit paid each month equals the monthly benefit amount of $2,000 minus the remaining balance of the RET charge. The RET charge for a given month cannot exceed the benefit for that month, but it may reduce the benefit to zero in some months. A partial benefit is paid if the remaining RET balance is less than the monthly benefit amount.		
January monthly benefit	$0a	$1,440b
February through June monthly benefits	$0a	$2,000
July monthly benefit	$1,320b	$2,000
August through December monthly benefits: full benefits paid	$2,000	$2,000, plus increase resulting from benefit recomputation at FRA to take into account months for which no benefit or a partial benefit was paid due to the RET

Source: Congressional Research Service.

Notes: In this example, it is assumed that the worker beneficiary receives benefits based on his or her own work record only. The starting benefit amounts are assumed to include reductions for retirement before FRA, and to exclude other reductions that may apply. The example has been constructed so that the year" provision does not apply, by assuming that the beneficiary both works and collects benefits over the full calendar year. (See "Grace Year" section.) Alternatively, under the grace year provision, a beneficiary who is in the first year of entitlement is not subject to the RET in any month during which he or she has earnings that do not exceed the monthly exempt amount (the annual exempt amount divided by 12), regardless of the beneficiary's total amount of earnings for the year.

[a] No benefit is paid this month because the beneficiary's RET balance is larger than the monthly benefit amount, so the RET charge for this month is equal to the benefit amount.

[b] A partial benefit is paid this month because the beneficiary's RET balance is smaller than the monthly benefit amount.

As discussed above, certain auxiliary benefits (benefits paid to the worker's family members such as a spouse or children) are subject to withholding under the RET if either the worker beneficiary or the auxiliary beneficiary has earnings above the exempt amount. When the worker beneficiary has earnings above the exempt amount, these earnings are charged against the total family benefit, that is, the total of benefits paid to the worker beneficiary and auxiliary beneficiaries who receive benefits based on the worker beneficiary's record. (When the auxiliary beneficiary has earnings above the exempt amount, these earnings are charged only against the auxiliary beneficiary's benefit, as discussed below.)

Table 3 provides an example of a worker beneficiary who is entitled to a monthly retirement benefit of $2,000 (this amount has already been adjusted for retirement before FRA). In addition, the worker beneficiary's spouse and child are each entitled to a monthly auxiliary benefit of $1,000 based on the worker beneficiary's record. Therefore, the total monthly family benefit is $4,000.[15]

If the worker beneficiary is below FRA and has earnings above the exempt amount, reductions under the RET are pro-rated among family members in proportion to each family member's original entitlement amount, before any adjustment for the family maximum or for retirement before FRA.[16] The total amount of the reduction remains the same, but the reduction is pro-rated across two or more people. If reductions under the RET are large enough to exceed the total family benefit for one or more months, no benefits are payable to the family for those months. If a partial benefit is payable for a given month, reflecting a reduction under the RET for that month that is less than the total family benefit, the partial benefit is pro-rated among family members.

In **Table 3**, benefits for the illustrative family are shown under two cases of the RET. The first case shows a family headed by a worker beneficiary who is below FRA throughout the calendar year and is subject to a benefit reduction under the RET equal to one-half of earnings above the lower exempt amount of $14,640 in 2012. The second case shows a family headed by a worker beneficiary who will attain FRA during the calendar year and is subject to a benefit reduction under the RET equal to one-third of earnings above the higher exempt amount of $38,880 in 2012.

Table 3. Application of the Retirement Earnings Test to a Family Consisting of a Worker Beneficiary with Earnings Above the Annual Exempt Amount and Auxiliary Beneficiaries (a Spouse and a Child), 2012

Step	Worker Beneficiary is Below FRA Throughout Calendar Year	Worker Beneficiary Will Attain FRA During Calendar Year
1. Social Security unreduced total monthly family benefit	$4,000	$4,000
of which:	of which:	of which:
Worker beneficiary's unreduced benefit	$2,000	$2,000
Spouse's unreduced benefit	$1,000	$1,000
Child's unreduced benefit	$1,000	$1,000
2. Calculation of worker beneficiary's earnings above the annual exempt amount		
Worker beneficiary's earnings in 2012	$40,000	$40,000
RET exempt amount in 2012	$14,640	$38,880
Worker beneficiary's earnings above the annual exempt amount	$25,360	$1,120
3. RET charge (= one-half of earnings above the exempt amount for worker beneficiary who is below FRA, or one-third of earnings above the exempt amount for worker beneficiary who will attain FRA during calendar year)	$12,680	$560

Step	Worker Beneficiary is Below FRA Throughout Calendar Year	Worker Beneficiary Will Attain FRA During Calendar Year
4. Application of the RET to the total family benefit. The total family benefit paid each month equals the monthly family benefit amount of $4,000 minus the remaining balance of the RET charge, where the RET charge is pro-rated across family members by original benefit amount (shown in notes to the table). The RET charge for a given month cannot exceed the total family benefit for that month, but it may reduce the family benefit to zero in some months. A partial benefit is paid if the remaining RET balance is less than the monthly family benefit amount.		
January total monthly family benefit	$0a	$3,440b
February and March total monthly family benefit	$0a	$4,000
April total monthly family benefit	$3,320c	$4,000
May through December total monthly family benefit	$4,000	$4,000, plus increase resulting from benefit recomputation at FRA to take into account months for which no benefit or a partial benefit was paid due to the RET

Source: Congressional Research Service.

Notes: In this example, it is assumed that the worker beneficiary receives benefits based on his or her own work record only, and that the spouse and child beneficiaries receive auxiliary benefits based on the worker beneficiary's record only. The starting benefit amounts are assumed to include reductions for retirement before FRA, and to exclude other benefit reductions that may apply, such as those related to receipt of a non-covered pension and the maximum family benefit amount. The example has been constructed so that the "grace year" provision does not apply, by assuming that the beneficiary both works and collects benefits over the full calendar year. (See "Grace Year" section.) Alternatively, under the grace year provision a beneficiary who is in the first year of entitlement is not subject to the RET in any month during which he or she has earnings that do not exceed the monthly exempt amount (the annual exempt amount divided by 12), regardless of the beneficiary's total amount of earnings for the year.

a No benefit is paid this month because the beneficiary's RET balance is larger than the monthly benefit amount, so the RET charge for this month is equal to the benefit amount.

b A partial benefit is paid to each family member in January because the RET balance is smaller than the total family benefit amount for the month. The RET balance of $560 is pro-rated and charged against all beneficiaries in proportion to their original entitlement amounts. One-half of the RET charge ($280) is applied to the worker beneficiary and one-fourth ($140) each is applied to the spouse and child. Therefore the worker beneficiary receives a January benefit of $1,720 ($2,000 - $280) and the spouse and child each receive January benefits of $860 ($1,000 - $140).

c A partial benefit is paid to each family member in April because the remaining RET balance is smaller than the total family benefit amount for the month. The remaining RET balance of $680 is pro-rated and charged against all beneficiaries in proportion to their original entitlement amounts. One-half of the RET charge ($340) is applied to the worker beneficiary and one-fourth ($170) each is applied to the spouse and child. Therefore the worker beneficiary receives an April benefit of $1,660 ($2,000 - $340) and the spouse and child each receive April benefits of $830 ($1,000 - $170).

The preceding examples illustrate cases in which the worker beneficiary has earnings above the exempt amount. In some cases, both the worker beneficiary and an auxiliary beneficiary (such as a spouse) may have earnings above the exempt amount. **Table 4** shows an example of a couple in which (1) one member, the worker beneficiary, receives a retired-worker benefit based on his or her own work record, and (2) one member, the auxiliary beneficiary, receives a spousal benefit only. Both beneficiaries are assumed to be below FRA throughout the calendar year and to have earnings above the RET exempt amount.[17] Because neither beneficiary will attain FRA during the calendar year, both are subject to the same RET exempt amount and benefit reduction rate. Benefit reductions under the RET are applied to the couple in the following order:[18]

- First, the worker beneficiary's RET charge is pro-rated and applied to both the worker beneficiary's retired-worker benefit and the auxiliary beneficiary's spousal benefit.[19]

- Second, if there is a balance remaining on the spousal benefit (if the spousal benefit has not been reduced to zero), the auxiliary beneficiary's RET charge is applied to (and further reduces) his or her spousal benefit only (the auxiliary beneficiary's earnings above the RET exempt amount do not affect the worker beneficiary's retired-worker benefit).

Table 4. Application of the Retirement Earnings Test to a Couple Consisting of a Worker Beneficiary and an Auxiliary (Spousal) Beneficiary, Both of Whom Have Earnings Above the Annual Exempt Amount and Are Below FRA Throughout the Calendar Year, 2012

Step	Spouse #1: Worker Beneficiary	Spouse #2: Auxiliary Beneficiary
1. Social Security retired-worker benefit, based on own work record	$2,000	
2. Social Security auxiliary (spousal) benefit		$1,000
3. Calculation of earnings above annual exempt amount		
Earnings in 2012	$25,000	$25,0
RET exempt amount in 2012	$14,640	$14,6
Earnings above annual exempt amount	$10,360	$10,3
4. RET charge (= one-half of earnings above the exempt amount for both worker beneficiary and auxiliary beneficiary, both of whom are below FRA throughout the calendar year)	$5,180	$5,180
5. Application of the RET		
January benefit: Worker beneficiary's RET charge is applied to total family benefits of $3,000.	$0	$0
February benefit: Balance of worker beneficiary's RET charge ($2,180 = $5,180 -$3,000) is pro-rated between worker beneficiary and auxiliary beneficiary in proportion to their original entitlement amount (a ratio of two to one): $1,453 is applied to the worker beneficiary and $727 is applied to the auxiliary beneficiary. In addition, $273 of auxiliary beneficiary's RET charge is applied to the auxiliary beneficiary's benefit only, reducing it to zero.	$547	$0
March through June monthly benefits: Worker beneficiary receives full monthly benefits. Auxiliary beneficiary's monthly benefit is reduced to zero by his or her own RET charge (worker beneficiary is not affected).	$2,000	$0

Table 4. (Continued)

Step	Spouse #1: Worker Beneficiary	Spouse #2: Auxiliary Beneficiary
July monthly benefit: Worker beneficiary receives full monthly benefit. Auxiliary beneficiary's RET balance of $907 ($5,180 -$4,273) is charged to his or her benefit.	$2,000	$93
August through December monthly benefits: full benefits paid to both spouses	$2,000	$1,000

Source: Congressional Research Service.

Notes: In this example, both beneficiaries are assumed to be below FRA throughout the calendar year and therefore are subject to the same RET exempt amount and benefit reduction rate. It is assumed that the worker beneficiary receives benefits based on his or her own work record only, and that the auxiliary beneficiary (spouse) receives benefits based on the worker beneficiary's record only. The starting benefit amounts are assumed to include reductions for retirement before FRA, and to exclude other benefit reductions that may apply, such as those related to receipt of a non-covered pension. The example has been constructed so that the "grace year" provision does not apply, by assuming that the beneficiaries both work and collect benefits over the full calendar year. (See "Grace Year" section.) Alternatively, under the grace year provision, a beneficiary who is in the first year of entitlement is not subject to the RET in any month during which he or she has earnings that do not exceed the monthly exempt amount (the annual exempt amount divided by 12), regardless of the beneficiary's total amount of earnings for the year.

More complex situations may exist in which, for example, a person is dually entitled to a retired-worker benefit (based on his or her own work record) and a spousal benefit (based on a different work record) and the person has earnings above the exempt amount. In the case of a dually-entitled beneficiary, his or her earnings above the exempt amount affect both his or her own retired-worker benefit and the spousal benefit that he or she receives. The dually entitled beneficiary's earnings above the exempt amount do not affect the retired-worker benefit received by his or her spouse because that benefit is based on the spouse's work record.

Table 5 summarizes the applicability of the RET to worker beneficiaries and auxiliary beneficiaries when either type of beneficiary has earnings above the exempt amount.

Table 5. Applicability of the Retirement Earnings Test to Worker Beneficiaries and Auxiliary Beneficiaries

Beneficiary Type	Worker Beneficiary Has Earnings Above the Exempt Amount	Auxiliary Beneficiary Has Earnings Above the Exempt Amount
Worker Beneficiary	Worker beneficiary's own benefit is reduced.	Only the auxiliary benefit is reduced, not the worker beneficiary's benefit.
Auxiliary Beneficiary: Spouse	Auxiliary benefits to spouses are reduced for the worker beneficiary's earnings above the exempt amount, which are charged against the total family benefit.	Only the auxiliary benefit is reduced, not the worker beneficiary's benefit.
Auxiliary Beneficiary: Divorced Spouse	A divorced spouse's benefit is not reduced for the worker beneficiary's earnings above the exempt amount if the couple has been divorced at least two years.	Only the auxiliary benefit is reduced, not the worker beneficiary's benefit.
Auxiliary Beneficiary: Child	Auxiliary benefits to children are reduced for the worker beneficiary's earnings above the exempt amount, which are charged against the total family benefit.	Only the auxiliary benefit is reduced, not the worker beneficiary's benefit.
Auxiliary Beneficiary: Mother or Father with Qualifying Child in Care (child under age 16 or disabled)	Not applicable (worker beneficiary is deceased).	The mother's or father's benefit is reduced.
Auxiliary Beneficiary: Widow(er)	Not applicable (worker beneficiary is deceased).	The widow(er)'s benefit is reduced.
Auxiliary Beneficiary: Parent	Not applicable (worker beneficiary is deceased).	The parent's benefit is reduced.

Source: Social Security Administration, *Social Security Handbook*, revised November 19, 2007, http://www.ssa.gov/OP_Home/handbook/handbook.18/handbook-1806.html.

Notes: A worker beneficiary's spouse or child who is receiving mother's/father's benefits or child's benefits based on a third person's work record is deemed entitled on the worker beneficiary's record. Therefore, the worker beneficiary's earnings above the exempt amount would be charged not only against his or her own benefits and the benefits of those entitled on his or her record, but also against the spouse's or child's benefits that are based on a third person's work record. As noted previously, disabled beneficiaries are subject to different rules and limitations regarding earnings.

POLICY ISSUES

Policymakers have asked questions about the RET's impact on labor supply and on the timing of Social Security benefit claims. Some argue that the RET is perceived as a "tax" on work effort, and that it induces workers to work fewer hours, or even to retire completely from the workforce. Another line of enquiry is whether the RET causes workers to delay claiming Social Security benefits. Both of these effects could have important implications for the retirement security of workers, their spouses and their survivors.

Quantitative studies have found mixed evidence concerning the RET's impact on work hours, retirement and the timing of Social Security benefit claims. Although the RET has been found to have a substantial effect on the labor supply of workers at or just above the annual RET threshold, the impact on workers with higher wages and salaries is more ambiguous. There is somewhat stronger evidence that the RET causes workers to delay claiming Social Security benefits.

The RET and Work Incentives

The impact of the RET on work hours varies by income level. At wages and salaries that are at or just above the annual RET threshold, the RET may encourage workers to work fewer hours, to keep wages or salaries just under the RET threshold. This effect is known as "bunching" or "clustering" under the RET threshold. A 1999 study found that a subset of workers do cluster at earnings levels just below the RET threshold.[20]

At higher earnings levels, the RET's impact on work hours is more ambiguous. Some workers perceive the RET as a tax on work effort (despite the recomputation of benefits at FRA). Moreover, other workers who are aware of the recomputation may place a relatively low value on future income. To the extent that the RET is perceived as a tax on earnings, it may induce some workers to reduce their work hours or even to retire completely from the workforce. Other workers, however, may respond to the RET reduction to Social Security benefits by working more, not fewer, hours to reach their income goals or requirements. For these workers, eliminating the RET would increase total income (income from labor plus income from Social Security). This has led some to argue that eliminating the RET would benefit some higher earners because the additional Social Security benefits that would become available would permit higher earners, if they wished, to reduce their work hours.

One study of the period from 1973 to 1998 found that the RET had little or no effect on the aggregate work hours and earnings of men aged 62 and older, although there is somewhat stronger evidence that the RET had an impact on women's earnings (no evidence was found for an impact on women's work hours).[21] However, a study of Social Security beneficiaries' response to the 2000 removal of the RET for beneficiaries at or above FRA found that, when workers are segmented by earnings level, fairly large effects on earnings are found, with the effects on earnings concentrated just below and above the RET threshold. (The study did not examine how work hours were affected by the 2000 change in the RET.)[22] Research has not found the RET to have a large effect on labor force participation, that is, a worker's decision to retire or remain in the workforce. This is perhaps in part because the RET is a relatively small part of the larger retirement decision that includes other factors such as pension rules and the worker's health, and also because it is difficult to separate the RET's impact from the trend toward later retirement that is already under way.

The RET and Incentives to Claim Social Security Benefits

Because the RET applies to persons who are younger than FRA, it may discourage persons below the FRA from claiming benefits. As noted earlier, some workers perceive the RET as a "tax" on benefits received before FRA, even though the recomputation of benefits at FRA (which results in a higher monthly benefit starting at FRA) allows the worker to recoup benefits withheld under the RET.

The quantitative evidence that the RET has an impact on the decision concerning when to claim Social Security benefits is somewhat stronger than the quantitative evidence for the RET's impact on work and earnings. For example, the Gruber and Orszag study that examined persons aged 62 and older during the period from 1973 to 1998 estimated that a $1,000 increase in the RET threshold could increase the share of men aged 62 and older who receive Social Security benefits by 0.7% to 1.6%, while eliminating the RET could increase that share by 5.2% to 13.5%.[23] A more recent study that examined the 2000 elimination of the RET for men and women at or above FRA found a 2 to 5 percentage point increase in benefit claims among men and women aged 65 to 69, and a 3 to 5 percentage point increase among men and women who reach the age of 65.[24]

The RET, Retirement Security and Early Benefit Claims

Some argue that, to the extent the RET causes some workers to delay claiming Social Security benefits, this can be beneficial for the worker as well as for his or her spouse or survivor. Claiming Social Security benefits before the FRA can reduce a worker's Social Security benefit amount in two ways, as noted earlier: (1) through the RET, although when the worker attains FRA his or her benefits are recomputed and a higher monthly benefit amount is payable starting at FRA; and (2) through the actuarial reduction for early retirement which, although it is intended to be actuarially fair to the individual over his or her expected lifetime, causes a permanent reduction to the worker's monthly Social Security benefit amount.

As discussed, the RET applies to spousal benefits. (See section "The RET May Affect Social Security Benefits Received by Spouses, Survivors and Other Dependents.") Spousal benefits that have been reduced by the RET are restored starting when the spouse attains FRA. Spousal benefits are not restored, however, when the RET is applied to the benefits of a spouse who is already at or above FRA. (See "Benefits Withheld Under the RET are Restored Starting at FRA.")

Survivors' benefits may be permanently affected by the worker beneficiary's decision to claim benefits before FRA. Under a provision in the Social Security Act called the *widow(er)'s limit provision*, the widow(er)'s benefit may be reduced if the widow(er)'s benefit payable on the worker's record exceeds the benefit the worker was receiving (including any actuarial reduction for early retirement that may have reduced the worker's benefit) before his or her death.[25] If a worker has benefits withheld under the RET and he or she dies before attaining FRA (when the worker's benefit would have been recomputed), for purposes of determining the limit on the widow(er)'s benefit, the worker's benefit is recomputed at the time of the worker's death to take into account months for which no benefit or a partial benefit was paid as a result of the RET.

Elderly widows, in particular, may face reduced living standards if their spouses claim benefits before FRA, because of the actuarial reduction to benefits described above. Women tend to outlive their husbands and are therefore more likely than men to receive Social Security survivors' benefits.

In addition, individuals and couples are more likely to deplete other assets later in retirement, leaving the couple or surviving spouse more reliant on Social Security.

Other Policy Issues

Some argue that eliminating the RET would have positive budget and economic effects because people would work more and pay more Social Security payroll and other taxes. The effect of the RET on labor supply is probably modest, however, as discussed above.

A common complaint among beneficiaries affected by the RET is that they are being denied a benefit they have "bought and paid for." A related argument is that the RET resembles a form of needs testing, making benefit receipt contingent on demonstrating "need" for this earned benefit. Supporters of the RET counter that Social Security is intended as a form of insurance against the risks of retirement and disability; just as the program does not pay disability benefits to those who are not disabled, it should not pay retirement benefits to those who are not retired.

The recomputation of benefits at FRA to restore benefits withheld under the RET is not widely known or understood. As noted previously, if a beneficiary has benefits withheld under the RET, his or her benefit is recomputed when he or she attains FRA to take into account months for which no benefit or a partial benefit was paid due to the RET. The recomputation results in a higher monthly benefit amount starting at FRA and allows the worker to recoup the value of any benefits "lost" under the RET, assuming he or she lives to average life expectancy. As a result, some observers argue that the RET should not be perceived as a "tax."[26] However, for some workers with shorter lifespans, the recovery of benefits may be incomplete. Conversely, for those who live longer than average, the recomputation may result in higher lifetime benefits that more than make up for the initial benefit reductions under the RET. Because life expectancy is linked to income, some argue that the RET may be regressive on a lifetime basis.[27]

Critics of the RET argue that it discriminates against claimants who must continue working to supplement their benefits. In contrast, claimants with no earnings who have other forms of income, such as private pensions or investment income, can receive full Social Security benefits. Supporters of the RET counter that eliminating the RET would provide a bonus to people who are fortunate enough to be able to continue working after becoming entitled to retirement benefits, and the additional Social Security benefits may allow or encourage some individuals to reduce their work hours.

FINANCIAL EFFECT OF REPEALING THE RET ON THE SOCIAL SECURITY TRUST FUND

Under current law, the RET has no major effect on Social Security financing over the long run because, *on average*, the RET has "no significant effect" on lifetime benefits.[28] Therefore, the Social Security Administration's Office of the Chief Actuary (OCACT) estimates that elimination of the RET for individuals aged 62 or older would have no major effect on Social Security's projected long-range financial outlook.[29]

In the short run, however, OCACT estimates that elimination of the RET would have a negative effect on the Social Security trust fund in the amount of $81 billion from 2012 to 2018. The trust fund would experience a projected cash-flow deficit of $12.1 billion in 2012, and a projected cash-flow deficit of $10.4 billion in 2018. OCACT notes: "In the first several years after elimination of the retirement earnings test, benefit payments are projected to increase substantially, because benefits are paid under the proposal where such payments would be withheld, or the individual would have not applied for benefits yet, under current law."[30]

In summary, OCACT notes that the projected financial effects for the Social Security program of eliminating the RET are due to "(1) some individuals no longer having their benefits withheld, (2) some individuals who would apply for Social Security benefits earlier because of the earnings test elimination, and (3) a small net increase in earnings for individuals currently subject to the earnings test."[31]

APPENDIX A. COMPUTATION OF THE SOCIAL SECURITY RETIRED-WORKER BENEFIT

To be eligible for a Social Security retired-worker benefit, a person generally needs 40 earnings credits, or 10 years of Social Security-covered employment (among other requirements). A worker's initial monthly benefit is based on his or her 35 highest years of earnings which are indexed to historical wage growth (earnings through the age of 60 are indexed; earnings thereafter are counted at nominal value). The 35 highest years of indexed earnings are divided by 35 to determine the worker's career-average annual earnings. The resulting amount is divided by 12 to determine the worker's average indexed monthly earnings (AIME). If a worker has fewer than 35 years of earnings in covered employment, years of no earnings are entered as zeros.

The worker's basic benefit amount (i.e., before any adjustments for early or delayed retirement) is the primary insurance amount (PIA). The PIA is determined by applying a formula to the AIME as shown in **Table A-1**. First, the AIME is sectioned into three brackets, or levels, of earnings. Three progressive factors—90%, 32%, and 15%—are applied to the three different brackets of AIME. The three products derived from multiplying each factor and bracket of AIME are added together. For workers who become eligible for retirement benefits (i.e., those who attain age 62), become disabled, or die in 2012, the PIA is determined as shown in the example in **Table A-1**.

Table A-1. Computation of a Worker's Primary Insurance Amount in 2012 Based on an Illustrative AIME of $5,000

Factors	Three Brackets of AIME (2012)	PIA for Worker with an Illustrative AIME of $5,000
90%	first $767 of AIME, plus	$690.30
32%	AIME over $767 and through $4,624, plus	$1,234.20
15%	AIME over $4,624	$56.40
Total Worker's PIA (rounded down)		$1,980.00

Source: Congressional Research Service.

Adjustment to Benefits Claimed Before or After FRA

A worker's initial monthly benefit is equal to his or her PIA if he or she begins receiving benefits at FRA (i.e., FRA is the earliest age at which full (unreduced) retirement benefits are payable). A worker's initial monthly benefit will be *less* than his or her PIA if he or she begins receiving benefits *before* FRA, and it will be *greater* than his or her PIA if he or she begins receiving benefits *after* FRA. As noted previously, FRA ranges from the age of 65 to 67 depending on the person's year of birth.

Retirement benefits are reduced by five-ninths of 1% (or 0.0056) of the worker's PIA for each month of entitlement before FRA up to 36 months, for a reduction of about 6.7% a year. For each month of benefit entitlement before FRA in excess of 36 months, retirement benefits are reduced by five-twelfths of 1% (or 0.0042), for a reduction of 5% a year. Workers who delay filing for benefits until after FRA receive a delayed retirement credit (DRC). The DRC applies beginning with the month the worker attains FRA and ending with the month before he or she attains the age of 70. Starting in 1990, the DRC increased until it reached 8% per year for workers born in 1943 or later (i.e., starting with those who attained age 62 in 2005 or age 66 in 2009).[32]

APPENDIX B. SOCIAL SECURITY AUXILIARY BENEFITS (BENEFITS FOR THE WORKER'S FAMILY MEMBERS)

Social Security provides benefits to eligible family members of a retired, disabled or deceased worker. Benefits payable to family members are equal to a specified percentage of the worker's PIA, subject to a maximum family benefit amount.

Social Security provides a monthly benefit to the spouse or divorced spouse (if the marriage lasted 10 or more years) of an entitled retired or disabled worker equal to 50% of the worker's PIA.[33] A monthly survivor benefit equal to 100% of the deceased worker's PIA is payable to the surviving spouse or surviving divorced spouse of a worker who was fully insured at the time of death.[34] Benefits for spouses, divorced spouses and surviving spouses are reduced if claimed before FRA. In addition, these benefits are reduced or fully offset if the beneficiary receives his or her own Social Security retired-worker benefit or a pension from a job that was not covered by Social Security (such as certain federal, state or local government jobs).

The child of a disabled or retired worker is eligible for 50% of the worker's PIA. The child of a deceased worker is eligible for 75% of the worker's PIA.[35] Social Security also provides a monthly mother's or father's benefit, equal to 75% of the worker's PIA, to a surviving parent of any age who cares for the deceased worker's child, when that child is under the age of 16 or disabled.

Table B-1 provides a summary of Social Security auxiliary benefits for the family of a retired, disabled or deceased worker, including eligibility requirements related to age and other factors.

Maximum Family Benefit Amount

The total amount of benefits payable to a family based on a retired or deceased worker's record is capped by the maximum family benefit amount. The maximum family benefit varies from 150% to 188% of the retired or deceased worker's PIA, and the maximum family benefit cannot be exceeded regardless of the number of beneficiaries entitled to benefits on the worker's record. If the sum of all benefits based on the worker's record exceeds the maximum family benefit amount, each dependent's or survivor's benefit is reduced in equal proportion to bring the total amount of benefits within the family maximum. For the family of a worker who attains age 62 in 2012, or dies in 2012 before attaining age 62, the total amount of benefits payable is limited to

- 150% of the first $980 of PIA, plus
- 272% of PIA over $980 and through $1,415, plus
- 134% of PIA over $1,415 and through $1,845, plus
- 175% of PIA over $1,845.

The dollar amounts in the maximum family benefit formula are indexed to average wage growth, as in the primary benefit formula. A separate maximum family benefit formula applies to the family of a worker who is entitled to disability benefits.

Table B-1. Social Security Auxiliary Benefits

Basis for Entitlement	Basic Eligibility Requirements	Basic Benefit Amount Before Any Adjustments
Spouse	At least age 62 The worker on whose record benefits are based must be receiving benefits.	50% of worker's PIA
Divorced Spouse (if divorced individual was married to the worker for at least 10 years before the divorce became final and is currently unmarried)	At least age 62 Generally, the worker on whose record benefits are based must be receiving benefits. However, a divorced spouse may receive benefits on the worker's record if the worker is eligible for (but not receiving) benefits and the divorce has been final for at least two years.	50% of worker's PIA

Table B-1. (Continued)

Basis for Entitlement	Basic Eligibility Requirements	Basic Benefit Amount Before Any Adjustments
Widow(er) & Divorced Widow(er) (if divorced individual was married to the worker for at least 10 years before the divorce became final and did not remarry before age 60)	At least age 60	100% of worker's PIA
Disabled Widow(er) & Divorced Disabled Widow(er) (if divorced individual was married to the worker for at least 10 years before the divorce became final and did not remarry before age 50)	At least age 50 The qualifying disability must have occurred: (1) before or within seven years of the worker's death; or (2) within seven years of having been previously entitled to benefits on the worker's record as a widow(er) with a child in his or her care; or (3) within seven years of having been previously entitled to benefits as a disabled widow(er) that ended because the qualifying disability ended (whichever is later).	100% of worker's PIA
Mothers and Fathers	Surviving parent of any age who cares for the deceased worker's child, when that child is either under the age of 16 or disabled. Eligibility generally ceases if the surviving mother or father remarries.	75% of deceased worker's PIA (subject to the maximum family benefit amount)
Parents	At least age 62 and has not married since the worker's death. The parent must have been receiving at least one-half of his or her support from the worker at the time of the worker's death or, if the worker had a period of disability which continued until death, at the beginning of the period of disability.	If one parent is entitled to benefits: 82.5% of deceased worker's PIA If two parents are entitled to benefits: 75% of deceased worker's PIA (for each) (subject to the maximum family benefit amount)

Basis for Entitlement	Basic Eligibility Requirements	Basic Benefit Amount Before Any Adjustments
Child	A child (including a dependent, unmarried biological child, adopted child, stepchild, and, in some cases, grandchild) of a retired, disabled, or deceased worker who was fully or currently insured at the time of death. The child must be: (1) under age 18; or (2) a full-time elementary or secondary student under age 19; or (3) a disabled person aged 18 or older whose disability began before age 22.	50% of worker's PIA for child of a retired or disabled worker 75% of deceased worker's PIA for child of a deceased worker (subject to the maximum family benefit amount)

Source: Congressional Research Service.

Notes: The maximum family benefit may apply, reducing the benefit received by each family member on a proportional basis. The maximum family benefit varies from 150% to 188% of a retired or deceased worker's PIA. For the family of a worker who is entitled to disability benefits, the maximum family benefit is the lesser of 85% of the worker's AIME or 150% of the worker's PIA, but no less than 100% of the worker's PIA.

APPENDIX C. ANNUAL EXEMPT AMOUNTS UNDER THE SOCIAL SECURITY RETIREMENT EARNINGS TEST, CALENDAR YEARS 2000-2012

The RET annual exempt amount is indexed to average wage growth in the economy. An exception, however, is that the annual exempt amount is not increased in a year during which no Social Security cost-of-living adjustment (COLA) is payable. In 2010 and 2011 there was no Social Security COLA, therefore the RET exempt amount did not increase in these years.

The RET applies only to wage and salary income (i.e., earnings from work). It does not apply to "unearned" income, such as income from pensions, rents, dividends, or interest.

Table C-1. Annual Exempt Amounts Under the Social Security
Retirement Earnings Test, Calendar Years 2000-2012

Calendar Year	Prior to Year of Attaining FRA	During Year of Attaining FRA
2000	$10,080	$17,000
2001	$10,680	$25,000
2002	$11,280	$30,000
2003	$11,520	$30,720
2004	$11,640	$31,080
2005	$12,000	$31,800
2006	$12,480	$33,240
2007	$12,960	$34,440
2008	$13,560	$36,120
2009	$14,160	$37,680
2010	$14,160	$37,680
2011	$14,160	$37,680
2012	$14,640	$38,880

Source: Social Security Administration, http://www.socialsecurity.gov/OACT/COLA /rtea.html.

End Notes

[1] The Social Security FRA is increasing gradually from age 65 to age 67 for workers born in 1938 or later; it will reach age 67 for workers born in 1960 or later. The FRA is 66 for workers who attain age 62 in 2012 (workers born in 1950) and workers who attain age 65 in 2012 (workers born in 1947). A person who claims benefits at FRA will receive full (unreduced) benefits. Workers may claim retirement benefits as early as age 62; however, a worker who claims benefits before FRA is subject to an actuarial reduction to benefits for early retirement that is unrelated to the RET.

[2] The Social Security Administration defines "excess earnings," for people who are below FRA and will not attain FRA during the calendar year, as 50% of earnings above the annual exempt amount. For people who will attain FRA during the calendar year, "excess earnings" are defined as 33 1/3% of earnings above the annual exempt amount (20 C.F.R. §404.430(b)). This definition is helpful for understanding the method of charging excess earnings against monthly benefits as described in the regulations (20 C.F.R. §404.434(b)).

[3] Committee on Economic Security, *Report of the Committee on Economic Security*, Washington, DC, January 1935, http://www.socialsecurity.gov/history in the section entitled "Contributory Annuities (Compulsory System): Outline of Plan."

[4] P.L. 74-271, the Social Security Act of 1935, §202(d), http://www.ssa.gov/history/35actii.html# Old-Benefit.

[5] P.L. 76-379, the Social Security Act Amendments of 1939, §203(d)(1) and §203(e), http://www.socialsecurity.gov/ history/pdf/1939Act.pdf.

[6] For workers who claim benefits before FRA, the monthly benefit amount is decreased by an adjustment that is roughly actuarially fair. The purpose of the actuarial reduction is to ensure that the worker receives roughly the same total lifetime benefits regardless of when he or she claims benefits between age 62 and FRA (assuming he or she lives to average life expectancy). Benefits taken before FRA are reduced about 6.7% per year for the first three years of benefit entitlement before FRA (i.e., the first 36 months from age 62 to age 65) and 5% per year thereafter. For example, for a worker whose FRA is 66, claiming benefits at age 62 results in an initial monthly benefit that is 25% lower than his or her PIA ((6.7% * 3 years) + (5% * 1 year)). Workers who delay filing for benefits until after FRA receive a delayed retirement credit (DRC). The DRC applies beginning with the month the worker attains FRA and ending with the month before he or she attains age 70. Starting in 1990, the DRC increased until it reached 8% per year for workers born in 1943 or later (i.e., starting with those who attained age 62 in 2005 or age 66 in 2009).

[7] Beneficiaries of Social Security Disability Insurance (SSDI) are subject to different rules and limitations regarding earnings. The limitations on earnings for SSDI beneficiaries are referred to as substantial gainful activity (SGA) amounts. The SGA differs from the RET in that a disability beneficiary whose earnings exceed the SGA threshold, after a trial work period, will lose eligibility for Social Security disability benefits. By contrast, a person whose earnings exceed the annual RET threshold may receive partial or full Social Security benefits for any months of the year after the RET charge has been applied. In addition, the benefit recomputation at FRA results in an upward adjustment of the Social Security benefit amount to reflect any months in which benefits were withheld in full or in part under the RET. In 2012, the SGA amount for non-blind beneficiaries is $1,010 a month (net of impairment-related work expenses). For blind beneficiaries, the SGA amount is $1,690 a month. Both amounts generally increase with the increase in average wages. For purposes of SSDI, a "disability" is defined as the inability to engage in substantial gainful activity by reason of a medically determinable physical or mental impairment expected to result in death or last at least 12 months. For more information, see CRS Report RL32279, *Primer on Disability Benefits: Social Security Disability Insurance (SSDI) and Supplemental Security Income (SSI)*, by Umar Moulta-Ali.

[8] Beneficiaries who will attain FRA during the calendar year are treated differently as a result of a compromise reached when the RET structure was modified in 2000. Before 2000, there were two RETs, one for beneficiaries below FRA and one for beneficiaries between FRA and age 70. The RET for beneficiaries between FRA and age 70 was more generous; the exempt amount was higher and the reduction to benefits was $1 for each $3 of earnings above that amount. By comparison, the RET for beneficiaries below FRA applied a lower exempt amount and the reduction to benefits was $1 for each $2 of earnings above that amount. In 2000, when Congress eliminated the RET for beneficiaries beginning with the month they attain FRA, there was a concern that beneficiaries who would attain FRA in 2000 would be worse off. The concern arose because, under pre-2000 law, the more generous RET applied to beneficiaries starting in January of the year they attained FRA. Therefore, eliminating the more generous RET would cause these beneficiaries to be subject to the lower exempt amount and the 50% offset during that year. To address this concern, the House version of the legislation, for 2000 only, allowed beneficiaries attaining FRA in 2000 to be subject to the more generous RET in the months preceding attainment of FRA. A Senate Manager's Amendment extended this provision to all future beneficiaries for the

year they attain FRA. In April 2000, President Clinton signed the legislation, which became P.L. 106-182.

[9] The annual exempt amounts are not increased in a year during which no Social Security cost-of-living adjustment is payable.

[10] The dually entitled beneficiary's earnings above the exempt amount will not affect the retired-worker benefit received by the worker on whose record the spousal benefit is based.

[11] In addition, if a beneficiary continues to work, the Social Security Administration automatically checks the person's record each year to determine if the additional earnings will increase his or her monthly benefit. For example, earnings for 2012 would be included in a recomputation effective January 2013. See Social Security Administration, *Program Operations Manual System* (Washington, DC), RS 00605.401, http://policy.ssa.gov/poms.nsf/links/0300605401.

[12] Under current law, the maximum reduction for early retirement ranges from 20% for a worker whose FRA is 65 to 30% for a worker whose FRA is 67.

[13] To simplify the example, it is assumed that the person was born on January 1. Therefore, there is no need to take into account the different annual exempt amount and benefit reduction rate that apply during the calendar year in which a beneficiary attains FRA. It is also assumed that the person both works and collects benefits over each full calendar year, so the "grace year" provision does not apply.

[14] For example, a person who has earnings of $26,640 in 2012 (i.e., $12,000 above the exempt amount) and a monthly Social Security benefit of $1,000 (or $12,000 in annual benefits) would be subject to a 50% reduction in Social Security benefits in 2012 under the RET. The person's benefits would be fully withheld for the first six months of 2012.

[15] A family's total benefits are subject to a cap known as the "family maximum," as discussed in Appendix B. For purposes of illustration, this example is simplified and does not include the family maximum.

[16] Social Security Administration, *Program Operations Manual System* (Washington, DC), RS 02501.110, http://policy

[17] An example of such a couple would be a worker beneficiary who receives a retired-worker benefit based on his or her own work record and an auxiliary beneficiary (a spouse) who is currently working but does not receive his or her own retired-worker benefit. This may be the case, for example, because the auxiliary beneficiary (the spouse) does not have enough Social Security-covered employment to qualify for a retirement benefit.

[18] 20 C.F.R. §404.434(b)(3).

[19] If the auxiliary beneficiary in this example (spouse #2) were dually entitled to a retired-worker benefit based on his or her own work record and a spousal benefit, the worker beneficiary's RET charge would apply only to the spousal benefit, and not the retired-worker benefit, received by spouse #2.

[20] Leora Friedberg, *The Labor Supply Effects of the Social Security Earnings Test*, National Bureau of Economic Research, Working Paper No. 7200, Cambridge, MA, June 1999, http://www.nber.org/papers/w7200.

[21] Jonathan Gruber and Peter Orszag, *Does the Social Security Earnings Test Affect Labor Supply and Benefits Receipt?*, National Bureau of Economic Research, Working Paper No. 7923, Cambridge, MA, September 2000, http://www.nber.org/papers/w7923.

[22] Jae G. Song and Joyce Manchester, "How Have People Responded to Changes in the Retirement Earnings Test in 2000," *Social Security Bulletin*, vol. 67, no. 1 (2007), http://www.ssa.gov/policy

[23] Jonathan Gruber and Peter Orszag, *Does the Social Security Earnings Test Affect Labor Supply and Benefits Receipt?*, National Bureau of Economic Research, Working Paper No. 7923, Cambridge, MA, September 2000, http://www.nber.org/papers/w7923.

[24] Jae G. Song and Joyce Manchester, "How Have People Responded to Changes in the Retirement Earnings Test in 2000," *Social Security Bulletin*, vol. 67, no. 1 (2007), http://www.ssa.gov/policy

[25] Under the *widow(er)'s limit provision,* the widow(er)'s benefit is limited to the higher of: (1) the benefit the worker would be receiving if he or she were still alive and (2) 82.5% of the worker's PIA. For more information, see David A. Weaver, *The Widow(er)'s Limit Provision of Social Security,* Social Security Administration, Office of Policy, Research, Evaluation and Statistics, Working Paper Series Number 92, June 2001.

[26] Adam Paul, "The Tax That Wasn't," *The American: The Journal of the American Enterprise Institute*, December 17, 2009, http://blog.american.com/?p=8363.

[27] Jonathan Gruber and Peter Orszag, *What To Do About The Social Security Earnings Test?*, Center for Retirement Research, Boston, MA, July 1999, p. 5, http://crr.bc.edu/images 43ac483c4de9t51d9eb41.

[28] Social Security Administration, Office of the Chief Actuary, *Estimated Long-Range OASDI Financial Effect of Repealing the Retirement Earnings Test at Ages 62 and Later*, April 30, 2010, p. 1 (hereinafter *SSA Cost Estimate for Repeal of the RET*).

[29] *SSA Cost Estimate for Repeal of the RET.* The estimate assumes that the RET would be eliminated starting in 2012 and is based on the intermediate assumptions of the 2009 Social Security Trustees Report. OCACT estimates that the policy change would reduce Social Security's projected long-range (average 75-year) funding shortfall from an amount equal to 2.00% of taxable payroll to an amount equal to 1.99% of taxable payroll.

[30] *SSA Cost Estimate for Repeal of the RET*, p. 2.

[31] *SSA Cost Estimate for Repeal of the RET*, p. 1.

[32] Other benefit adjustments may apply, such as those related to simultaneous entitlement to more than one type of Social Security benefit, receipt of a pension from work that was not covered by Social Security (a non-covered pension), the Social Security maximum family benefit, and the Social Security Retirement Earnings Test which is the focus of this report. For more information on the various benefit adjustments, see House Ways and Means Committee, 2008 Green Book, §1, Social Security: The Old-Age, Survivors, and Disability Insurance (OASDI) Programs, pp. 1-59 to 1-68, http://waysandmeans.house.gov/media /pdf/111/ssgb.pdf.

[33] The qualifying spouse must be at least age 62 or have a qualifying child (a child who is under age 16 or disabled) in his or her care. A spouse's benefit is reduced if he or she begins receiving benefits before FRA.

[34] The surviving spouse must be at least age 60 (or at least age 50 if disabled) and must not have remarried before age 60 (or age 50 if disabled).

[35] The child must be (1) under age 18; or (2) a full-time elementary or secondary student under age 19; or (3) a disabled person aged 18 or older whose disability began before age 22.

In: Social Security Benefits   ISBN: 978-1-63321-828-4
Editor: Juliana Lawrence   © 2014 Nova Science Publishers, Inc.

Chapter 3

SOCIAL SECURITY: THE WINDFALL ELIMINATION PROVISION (WEP)*

Christine Scott

SUMMARY

The windfall elimination provision (WEP) reduces the Social Security benefits of workers who also have pension benefits from employment not covered by Social Security. Its purpose is to remove an advantage or "windfall" these workers would otherwise receive as a result of the interaction between the Social Security benefit formula and the workers' relatively short careers in Social Security-covered employment. Opponents contend the provision is basically imprecise and can be unfair.

BACKGROUND

The Social Security benefit formula is designed so that workers with low average lifetime earnings in Social Security-covered employment receive a benefit that is a larger proportion of their earnings than do workers with high average lifetime earnings. The benefit formula does not distinguish, however, between workers who have low average earnings because they worked for

---

* This is an edited, reformatted and augmented version of a Congressional Research Service publication 98-35, prepared for Members and Committees of Congress, dated February 15, 2013.

many years at low wages in Social Security-covered employment and workers who have low average earnings because they worked briefly in Social Security-covered employment. The generous benefit that would be provided to workers with short careers in Social Security-covered employment—in particular, workers who have split their careers between Social Security-covered and non-covered employment—is sometimes referred to as a "windfall" that would exist in the absence of the windfall elimination provision (WEP). The WEP reduces the Social Security benefits of workers who also have pension benefits from employment not covered by Social Security.

A worker is eligible for Social Security after he or she works in Social Security-covered employment for 10 or more years (40 or more quarters). The worker's earning history is indexed to wage growth to bring earlier years of his or her earnings up to a comparable, current basis. Average indexed earnings are found by totaling the highest 35 years of indexed wages and then dividing by 35. Next, a monthly average, known as Average Indexed Monthly Earnings (AIME), is found by dividing the annual average by 12.

The Social Security benefit formula is designed to provide a progressive benefit. The benefit formula applies three progressive factors—90%, 32%, and 15%—to three different levels, or brackets, of AIME.[1] The result is known as the "primary insurance amount" (PIA) and is rounded down to the nearest 10 cents. For persons who reach age the age of 62, die, or become disabled in 2013, the PIA is determined in *Table 1* as follows:

Table 1. Social Security Benefit Formula in 2013

Factor	Average Indexed Monthly Earnings
90%	of the first $791, plus
32%	of AIME over $791 and through $4,768, plus
15%	of AIME over $4,768

The averaging provision in the benefit formula tends to cause workers with short careers in Social Security-covered employment to have low AIMEs, similar to persons who worked for low wages in covered employment throughout their careers. This is because years of zero covered earnings are entered as zeros into the formula that averages the worker's wage history over 35 years. For example, a person with 10 years in Social Security-covered employment would have an AIME that reflects 25 years of zero earnings.

Consequently, for a worker with a low AIME because she split her career between covered and non-covered employment, the benefit formula replaces more of covered earnings at the 90% rate than if this worker had spent his or her full 35-year career in covered employment at the same wage level. The higher replacement rate[2] for workers who have split their careers between Social Security-covered and non-covered jobs is sometimes referred to as a "windfall."[3]

A different Social Security benefit formula, referred to as the "windfall elimination provision," applies to many workers who are entitled to Social Security as well as to a pension from work not covered by Social Security (e.g., individuals who work for certain state and local governments, or under the Federal Civil Service Retirement System).[4] Under these rules, the 90% factor in the first bracket of the formula is replaced by a factor of 40%. The effect is to lower the proportion of earnings in the first bracket that are converted to benefits. *Table 2* illustrates how the regular and WEP provisions work in 2013.

**Table 2. Monthly PIA for a Worker With Average
Indexed Monthly Earnings of $1,500
and Retiring in 2013**

Regular Formula		Windfall Elimination Formula	
90% of first $791	$711.90	40% of first $791	$316.40
32% of earnings over $791 and through $4,768	$226.88	32% of earnings over $791 and through $4,768	$226.88
15% over $4,768	0.00	15% over $4,768	0.00
Total	$938.78	Total	$543.28

Source: Calculations were made by the Congressional Research Service (CRS).
Note: To simplify the example, rounding conventions that would normally apply are not used here.

Under the WEP formula, the benefit for the worker is reduced by $395.50 ($938.78 - $543.28) per month relative to the regular benefit formula. Note that the WEP reduction is limited to the first bracket in the AIME formula (90% vs. 40% formula rates), while the 32% and 15% factors for the second and third brackets are the same as in the regular benefit formula. As a result, for AIME amounts that exceed the first formula threshold of $791, the amount of the WEP reduction remains a flat $395.50 per month. For example, if the worker had an AIME of $4,000 instead of $1,500, the WEP reduction would still be $395.50 per month. The WEP therefore causes a proportionally larger reduction in benefits for workers with lower AIMEs and monthly benefit amounts. [5]

A "guarantee" in the WEP provision ensures that a worker's WEP reduction cannot exceed more than one half of the government pension based on the worker's non-covered work. This "guarantee" is designed to help protect workers with low non-covered pensions and also ensures that the WEP can never completely eliminate a worker's Social Security benefit. The WEP also exempts workers who have 30 or more years of "substantial" employment covered under Social Security, with lesser reductions for workers with 21 through 29 years of substantial covered employment, as shown in *Table 3*.[6]

Table 3. WEP Reduction Falls
with Years of Substantial Coverage

				Years of Social Security Coverage						
20	21	22	23	24	25	26	27	28	29	30
First factor in formula:										
40%	45%	50%	55%	60%	65%	70%	75%	80%	85%	90%
Maximum dollar amount of monthly WEP reduction in 2013:[a]										
$395.50	$355.95	$316.40	$276.85	$237.30	$197.75	$158.20	$118.65	$79.10	$39.55	$0.00

Source: Social Security Administration, How the Windfall Elimination Provision Can Affect Your Social Security Benefit, Washington, DC, http://www.socialsecurity.gov/retire2/wep-chart.htm.

[a] WEP reduction may be lower than the amount shown because the reduction is limited to one-half of the worker's pension from non-covered employment.

The WEP does *not* apply to (1) an individual who on January 1, 1984, was an employee of a government or nonprofit organization and to whom Social Security coverage was mandatorily extended by the 1983 amendments to the Social Security Act (e.g., the President, Members of Congress in office on December 31, 1983); (2) benefits for survivors; (3) workers who reached the age of 62, became disabled, or were first eligible for a pension from non-covered employment, before 1986; (4) benefits from foreign Social Security systems that are based on a "totalization" agreement with the United States; and (5) people whose only non-covered employment that resulted in a pension was in military service before 1957 or is based on railroad employment.

WHO IS AFFECTED BY THE WEP?

According to the Social Security Administration (SSA), as of December 2012, about 1.5 million Social Security beneficiaries were affected by the WEP, as shown in *Table 4*. About 1.4 million people (92.2%) affected by the WEP were retired workers. About 2.4% of all Social Security beneficiaries (including disabled and spouse beneficiaries), and about 4.0% of all retired worker beneficiaries, were affected by the WEP in December 2012.[7] Of retired workers affected by the WEP, approximately 61.9% were men.[8]

Table 4. Number of Beneficiaries in Current Payment Status with Benefits Affected by Windfall Elimination Provision (WEP), by State and Type of Benefit, December 2012

State	Total	Type of Benefit		
		Retired Workers	Disabled Workers	Spouses and Children
Total	1,466,386	1,351,752	18,158	96,476
Alabama	17,558	15,885	351	1,322
Alaska	8,011	7,552	105	354
Arizona	27,104	25,150	299	1,655
Arkansas	9,947	9,213	206	528
California	196,310	182,284	2,114	11,912
Colorado	45,386	42,482	660	2,244
Connecticut	14,758	14,041	157	560
Delaware	3,328	3,129	47	152
District of Columbia	7,578	7,199	135	244
Florida	81,811	75,619	890	5,302
Georgia	42,455	39,885	544	2,026
Hawaii	8,986	8,277	76	633
Idaho	6,294	5,802	80	412
Illinois	77,033	72,956	633	3,444
Indiana	14,329	13,338	205	786
Iowa	7,604	7,111	79	414
Kansas	8,266	7,681	133	452
Kentucky	19,023	17,653	348	1,022
Louisiana	30,319	27,517	667	2,135
Maine	13,787	12,978	165	644

Table 4. (Continued)

| | | | Type of Benefit | |
State	Total	Retired Workers	Disabled Workers	Spouses and Children
Maryland	42,500	39,846	518	2,136
Massachusetts	53,649	50,892	705	2,052
Michigan	18,302	16,810	301	1,191
Minnesota	15,786	14,830	164	792
Mississippi	8,819	8,109	156	554
Missouri	31,285	29,619	434	1,232
Montana	5,260	4,859	69	332
Nebraska	4,901	4,617	41	243
Nevada	22,296	21,177	228	891
New Hampshire	6,507	6,073	128	306
New Jersey	20,650	19,008	376	1,266
New Mexico	11,853	10,721	167	965
New York	29,068	26,730	446	1,892
North Carolina	26,052	24,315	327	1,410
North Dakota	2,253	2,099	17	137
Ohio	107,264	100,431	1,233	5,600
Oklahoma	16,319	14,919	303	1,097
Oregon	14,349	13,364	141	844
Pennsylvania	32,825	30,250	540	2,035
Rhode Island	4,691	4,413	67	211
South Carolina	16,006	14,834	223	949
South Dakota	3,541	3,334	36	171
Tennessee	17,967	16,571	250	1,146
Texas	130,515	121,020	1,566	7,929
Utah	12,060	10,918	145	997
Vermont	2,367	2,197	22	148
Virginia	44,354	40,976	430	2,948
Washington	27,336	24,893	316	2,127
West Virginia	5,750	5,155	130	465
Wisconsin	11,027	10,328	120	579
Wyoming	2,175	2,028	29	118
Outlying areas and foreign countries	78,772	60,664	636	17,472

Source: Social Security Administration, Office of Research, Evaluation and Statistics, January 2013, unpublished Table B.

LEGISLATIVE HISTORY AND RATIONALE

The windfall elimination provision was enacted in 1983 as part of major amendments designed to shore up the financing of the Social Security program. The 40% WEP formula factor was the result of a compromise between a House bill that would have substituted a 61% factor for the regular 90% factor and a Senate proposal that would have substituted a 32% factor for the 90% formula.[9]

The purpose of the 1983 law was to remove an unintended advantage that the regular Social Security benefit formula provided to persons who also had pensions from non-Social Security-covered employment. The regular formula was intended to help workers who spent their lifetimes in low paying jobs, by providing them with a benefit that replaces a higher proportion of their earnings than the benefit that is provided to workers with high earnings. However, the formula could not differentiate between those who worked in low-paid jobs throughout their careers and other workers who appeared to have been low paid because they worked many years in jobs not covered by Social Security. Under the old law, workers who were employed for only a portion of their careers in jobs covered by Social Security—even highly paid ones—also received the advantage of the "weighted" formula. The windfall elimination formula is intended to remove this advantage for these workers.

Arguments for the Windfall Elimination Provision

Proponents of the measure say that it is a reasonable means to prevent payment of overgenerous and unintended benefits to certain workers who otherwise would profit from happenstance (i.e., the mechanics of the Social Security benefit formula). Furthermore, they maintain that the provision rarely causes hardship because by and large the people affected are reasonably well off because by definition they also receive government pensions from non-covered work. The guarantee provision ensures that the reduction in Social Security benefits cannot exceed half of the pension from non-covered work, which protects persons with small pensions from non-covered work. In addition, the impact of the WEP is reduced for workers who spend 21 to 29 years in Social Security-covered work and is eliminated for persons who spend 30 years or more in Social Security-covered work.

Arguments Against the Windfall Elimination Provision

Some opponents believe the provision is unfair because it substantially reduces a benefit that workers may have included in their retirement plans. Others criticize how the provision works. They say the arbitrary 40% factor in the windfall elimination formula is an imprecise way to determine the actual windfall when applied to individual cases.

The WEP's Impact on Low-Income Workers

The impact of the WEP on low-income workers has been the subject of debate. Jeffrey Brown and Scott Weisbenner (hereinafter referred to as "Brown and Weisbenner") point out two reasons why the WEP can be regressive.[10] First, because the WEP adjustment is confined to the first bracket of the benefit formula ($791 in 2013), it causes a proportionally larger reduction in benefits for workers with lower AIMEs and benefit amounts. Second, a high earner is more likely than a low earner to cross the "substantial work" threshold for accumulating years of covered earnings (in 2013 this threshold is $21,075 in Social Security-covered earnings); therefore, high earners are more likely to benefit from the provision that phases out of the WEP for persons with between 21 and 30 years of covered employment.

Brown and Weisbenner found that the WEP does reduce benefits disproportionately for lower-earning households than for higher-earning households. For some high-income households, applying the WEP to covered earnings even provides a higher replacement rate than if the WEP were applied proportionately to all earnings, covered and non-covered. Brown and Weisbenner also found that the WEP can also lead to large changes in Social Security replacement rates based on small changes in covered earnings, particularly when a small increase in covered earnings carries a person over the threshold for an additional year of substantial covered earnings, leading to a modification in the WEP formula.

SSA estimated that in 2000, 3.5% of recipients affected by the WEP had incomes below the poverty line. For comparison purposes, at that time 8.5% of all Social Security beneficiaries aged 65 and older had incomes below the poverty line and 11.3% of the general population had incomes below the poverty line.[11] A potential conclusion is that persons who are subject to the WEP, who by definition also have pensions from non-covered employment, face a somewhat reduced risk of poverty compared with other Social Security beneficiaries.

End Notes

[1] Both the annual earnings amounts over the worker's lifetime and the bracket amounts are indexed to national wage growth so that the Social Security benefit replaces the same proportion of wages for each generation.

[2] A worker's replacement rate is the ratio of his or her Social Security benefit to pre-retirement income.

[3] The WEP is sometimes confused with the Government Pension Offset (GPO), which reduces Social Security spousal benefits of a worker who also has a government pension based on work that was not covered by Social Security. For more information on the GPO, please refer to CRS Report RL32453, Social Security: The Government Pension Offset (GPO), by Christine Scott.

[4] Social Security Act §215(a)(7). Federal service where Social Security taxes are withheld (Federal Employees' Retirement System or CSRS Offset) is not affected by the WEP.

[5] For the worker shown in Table 2, with an AIME of $1,500 and a monthly benefit of $938.78 under the regular benefit formula in 2013, the WEP reduction of $395.50 represents a 42% cut to the regular formula monthly benefit amount. By comparison, a worker with an AIME of $4,000 would be entitled to a PIA of $1,738.78 under the 2013 regular benefit formula, and the same WEP reduction of $395.50 per month would represent a 23% reduction in this worker's monthly benefit amount (CRS calculations).

[6] For determining years of coverage after 1978 for individuals with pensions from non-covered employment, "substantial coverage" is defined as 25% of the "old law" (i.e., if the 1977 Social Security Amendments had not been enacted) Social Security maximum taxable wage base for each year in question. In 2013, the "old-law" taxable wage base is equal to $84,300, therefore to earn credit for one year of "substantial" employment under the WEP a worker would have to earn at least $21,075 in Social Security-covered employment.

[7] Social Security data on the Social Security beneficiary and retired worker populations are available from the Monthly Statistical Snapshot, December 2012, at http://www.socialsecurity.gov/policy/docs/quickfacts/stat_snapshot/index.html

[8] Social Security Administration, Office of Research, Evaluation and Statistics, January 2013, unpublished table W01.

[9] Conference Report to Accompany H.R. 1900, 98th Cong., March 24, 1983 (Washington: GPO, 1983), p. 120.

[10] Jeffrey R. Brown and Scott Weisbenner, The Distributional Effects of the Social Security Windfall Elimination Provision, NBER, Working Paper no. 18342, August 2012, http://www.nber.org/papers/w18342.

[11] These are the most recent estimates available. Poverty rates were calculated by David Weaver of the Social Security Administration's Office of Retirement Policy using the March 2001 Current Population Survey (CPS). Poverty status is taken directly from the CPS and is thus subject to errors in the reporting of income. The sample size for the WEP poverty rate is relatively small (230 cases) and only includes persons for whom SSA administrative records could be matched.

In: Social Security Benefits
Editor: Juliana Lawrence

ISBN: 978-1-63321-828-4
© 2014 Nova Science Publishers, Inc.

Chapter 4

SOCIAL SECURITY: THE GOVERNMENT PENSION OFFSET (GPO)*

Gary Sidor

SUMMARY

Social Security spousal benefits were established in the 1930s to help support wives who are financially dependent on their husbands. It has since become more common for both spouses in a couple to work, with the result that, in more cases, both members of a couple are entitled to Social Security or other government pensions based on their own work records. Social Security does not provide both a full retired-worker and a full spousal benefit to the same individual.

Two provisions are designed to reduce the Social Security spousal benefits of individuals who are not financially dependent on their spouses because they receive benefits based on their own work records. These are

- the "dual entitlement" rule, which applies to spouses who qualify for both (1) Social Security spousal benefits based on their spouses' work histories in Social Security-covered employment and (2) their own Social Security retired- or disabled-worker benefits, based on their own work histories in Social Security-covered employment; and

---

* This is an edited, reformatted and augmented version of a Congressional Research Service publication RL32453, prepared for Members and Committees of Congress, dated April 23, 2014.

- the Government Pension Offset (GPO), which applies to spouses who qualify for both (1) Social Security spousal benefits based on their spouses' work histories in Social Security-covered employment and (2) their own government pensions, based on their own work in government employment that was not covered by Social Security.

The GPO reduces Social Security spousal or widow(er)'s benefits by two-thirds of the pension from non-covered government employment. The GPO does not reduce the benefits of the spouse who was covered by Social Security.

Opponents contend that the GPO is imprecise and can be unfair. Defenders argue it is the best method currently available for preserving the spousal benefit's original intent of supporting financially dependent spouses and also for eliminating an unfair advantage for spouses working in non-Social Security-covered employment compared with spouses working in Social Security-covered jobs (who are subject to the dual entitlement rule).

BACKGROUND

Generally, Social Security spousal and survivor benefits are paid to the spouses of retired, disabled, or deceased workers covered by Social Security. The spousal benefit equals 50% of a retired or disabled worker's benefit and the survivor benefit equals 100% of a deceased worker's benefit.

Spousal benefits, which Congress created in 1939, are intended for individuals who are financially dependent on a working spouse. For this reason, but also because of the costs, Social Security does not provide both full worker and full spousal benefits to the same individual. For persons who qualify for both a Social Security worker benefit (retirement or disability) based on their own work history and a Social Security spousal benefit based on a spouse's work history, the "dual entitlement" rule effectively caps total benefits at the higher of the worker's own benefit or the spousal benefit. The Government Pension Offset (GPO) is analogous in purpose to the "dual entitlement" provision and applies to individuals who qualify for both a pension based on their own *non*-Social Security-covered government work and a Social Security spousal benefit based on a spouse's work in Social Security-covered employment.[1] The intent of the dual entitlement rule and the GPO is the same—to reduce the Social Security spousal benefits of individuals who are not financially dependent on their spouses because they receive their own retired-worker or disabled-worker Social Security benefits, or their non-Social Security pension benefits.

Social Security Covered and Non-Covered Work

A worker is "covered" by Social Security if he or she works in "covered" employment and pays into Social Security through the Federal Insurance Contributions Act (FICA) payroll tax. A worker is entitled to Social Security disabled- or retired-worker benefits after paying into Social Security for 10 years (more specifically, 40 or more quarters for which the worker has covered earnings). Approximately 93% of workers were covered by Social Security in 2014.[2] The majority of non-covered positions are held by government employees: most federal employees hired before 1984 and some state and local government employees. Nationwide, approximately 73% of state and local government employees are covered by Social Security.[3] However, coverage varies from state to state. For example, approximately 97% of state and local employees in New York are covered by Social Security, whereas less than 3% of state and local employees in Ohio, and about 4% in Massachusetts, are covered.[4]

The Dual Entitlement Rule and the GPO

The GPO is intended to approximate Social Security's dual entitlement rule. The intent of both provisions is to reduce the Social Security benefits of spouses or widow(er)s who are not financially dependent on their spouses because they receive retirement benefits based on their own work records.

Dual Entitlement Rule

In the absence of the dual entitlement rule, a couple with two earners covered by Social Security would receive two full primary benefits as well as two full spousal or widow(er)'s benefits. The Social Security dual entitlement rule requires that a beneficiary effectively receive the *higher* of the Social Security worker's benefit or of the spousal or widow(er)'s benefit, but not both. The total benefit received by a worker consists of his or her own worker benefit plus the excess of the spousal or widow(er)'s benefit (if any) over his or her own benefit—not the sum of the two benefits.[5] Expressed simply, the higher of the two benefits is paid.

Table 1 demonstrates how the Social Security dual entitlement rule is applied to spouses.

Table 1. Dual Entitlement Formula Applied to Spouses

	John	Mary
Social Security monthly worker benefit (based on worker's earnings record) Maximum Social Security monthly spousal benefit (based on spouse's earnings record, equal to 50% of the spouse's Social Security worker benefit)Actual Social Security spousal monthly benefit paid (subtract worker benefit from spousal benefit; $0 if worker benefit is larger) Total (worker and spousal) Social Security monthly benefits paid to John and Mary	$2,000 $450 $0$2,000	$900 $1,000 $100 $1,000

Source: Illustrative example provided by the Congressional Research Service (CRS).

In this example, both John and Mary have worked enough years in Social Security-covered positions (i.e., paid into Social Security) to qualify for Social Security retirement benefits. John has earned a monthly Social Security worker benefit equal to $2,000. His wife Mary has earned a monthly Social Security worker benefit equal to $900. Both Mary and John are also eligible for spousal benefits based on the other's earnings: John is eligible for a $450 monthly spousal benefit, and Mary is eligible for a $1,000 monthly spousal benefit. Under the dual entitlement rule, Mary's worker benefit of $900 must be subtracted from her potential $1,000 spousal benefit, and only the difference of $100 is paid as a spousal benefit. In total, Mary will receive $1,000 monthly—$900 as a Social Security worker benefit and $100 as a Social Security spousal benefit. John will not be paid a spousal benefit because his $2,000 worker benefit based on his own earnings is higher than and more than offsets the potential $450 spousal benefit. The Social Security benefits received by the couple total $3,000 per month.

If John were to predecease Mary, Mary would then be entitled to a monthly widow's benefit of up to 100% of John's monthly amount. Mary would continue to collect her own benefit of $900 monthly, and that amount would offset John's full monthly benefit amount of $2,000. Thus, Mary would receive a Social Security worker benefit of $900 and a Social Security widow's benefit of $1,100 ($2,000 - $900), for a total monthly benefit of $2,000.

Because most workers are in Social Security-covered employment, the dual entitlement scenario is more common than the GPO among two-earner couples. In 2012, approximately 6.8 million out of 36.7 million Social Security retired worker beneficiaries, or about 19%, were dually entitled.[6]

Government Pension Offset Formula

The Social Security spousal or widow(er)'s benefit of a person who also receives a pension from government employment (federal, state, or local) that was based on work *not covered* by Social Security is reduced by a provision known as the GPO. The GPO reduction to Social Security spousal and widow(er)'s benefits equals *two-thirds* of the pension from non-covered government employment. If the pension from non-covered work is sufficiently large in comparison to a person's Social Security spousal or widow(er)'s benefit, the GPO may eliminate the entire Social Security spousal or widow(er)'s benefit.

In December 2013, almost 615,000 Social Security beneficiaries (about 1% of all Social Security beneficiaries) had spousal or widow(er)'s benefits reduced by the GPO (this figure does not include persons who were eligible for spousal or widow(er)'s benefits but were deterred from filing for them because of the GPO).[7] The GPO has no effect on the amount of the Social Security benefit a worker may receive based on his or her own work in Social Security-covered employment, but it does limit the amount that can be paid to his or her spouse or widow(er) who has worked in non-Social Security-covered employment.

Table 2 provides an example of how the GPO is applied, assuming that John worked in Social Security-covered employment while Mary spent her full career in state or local government employment that was not covered by Social Security.

Table 2. GPO Formula for Spouses

	John	Mary
Social Security retired- or disabled-worker monthly benefit (based on worker's earnings record)	$2,000	N/A
Non-Social Security-covered (government) monthly pension	N/A	$900
Maximum Social Security spousal monthly benefit eligible to receive (based on spouse's earnings record, equal to 50% of the spouse's Social Security retired worker benefit)	N/A	$1,000

Table 2. (Continued)

	John	Mary
Reduction in Social Security spousal monthly benefit due to GPO (equals 2/3 of the non-Social Security-covered pension: $900*2/3=$600)	N/A	$600
Actual Social Security spousal monthly benefit paid (subtract 2/3 of non-Social Security-covered worker's pension from Social Security spousal benefit: $1,000–$600=$400)	N/A	$400
Total monthly retirement benefits paid to John (Social Security only) and Mary (Social Security plus pension from non-covered employment)	$2,000	$1,300

Source: Illustrative example provided by CRS.
Note: N/A means not applicable.

In this example, John worked enough years in Social Security-covered employment to qualify for a monthly Social Security retired-worker benefit of $2,000. His wife, Mary, is *not* eligible for a Social Security retired-worker benefit because she worked in a non-Social Security-covered government position and did not contribute to Social Security. Instead, Mary is eligible for a $900 government pension based on her work in a non-Social Security-covered position. Mary is also eligible for a Social Security *spousal* benefit of up to $1,000 based on John's work history. Under the GPO, Mary's potential Social Security spousal benefit is reduced by an amount equal to two-thirds of her non-Social Security-covered government pension (or $600), and the difference of $400 ($1,000 - $600) is paid to her as a Social Security spousal benefit. In total, Mary will receive retirement benefits of $1,300 per month: $900 from her non-covered pension and $400 as a Social Security spousal benefit.[8]

If John predeceased Mary, then two-thirds of her $900 non-covered pension ($600) would be used to offset the $2,000 Social Security benefit she would be eligible for as a widow based on John's worker benefit. She would receive a $1,400 monthly widow's benefit from Social Security (in addition to her $900 monthly non-covered pension benefit).

Table 3 highlights the differences between the dual entitlement rule and the GPO.

Table 3. Dual Entitlement Rule Compared with Government Pension Offset

Dual Entitlement Rule	Government Pension Offset
Applies to individuals who qualify for both (a) a Social Security worker benefit (retirement or disability) based on their own work history in Social Security-covered employment and (b) a Social Security spousal or widow(er)'s benefit based on their spouse's work history in Social Security-covered employment.	Applies to individuals who qualify for both (a) a government pension based on non-Social Security-covered government employment and (b) a Social Security spousal or widow(er)'s benefit based on a spouse's Social Security-covered employment The GPO reduces Social Security benefits that a person receives as a spouse or widow(er) if he or she also has a federal, state or local government pension based on work that was not covered by Social Security.
Dually-entitled beneficiaries effectively receive the higher of the worker benefit or the spousal or widow(er)'s benefit. Specifically, the Social Security dual entitlement rule requires that 100% of a Social Security retirement or disability benefit earned as a worker be subtracted from any Social Security spousal or widow(er)'s benefit on is eligible to receive. Only the difference, if any, is paid as a spousal or widow(er)'s benefit and is added to the beneficiary's own worker benefit.	The GPO reduction to Social Security spousal or widow(er)'s benefits is equal to two-thirds of the non-covered government pension.

Source: Table compiled by CRS.

RATIONALE AND LEGISLATIVE HISTORY

Spouses' Financial Dependence

The policy rationale for Social Security spousal benefits has been, since the creation of spousal benefits in the 1930s, to support spouses who are financially dependent on the working spouse. The dual entitlement rule has operated since 1939 as a gauge of financial dependence.

Parity Between Spouses Subject to the Dual Entitlement Rule and the GPO

The GPO is intended to place spouses and widow(er)s whose government employment *was not covered* by Social Security in approximately the same position as spouses whose jobs *were covered* by Social Security. Before the GPO was enacted in 1977, workers who received pensions from a government job not covered by Social Security could also receive full Social Security spousal or widow(er)'s benefits even though they were not financially dependent on their spouses. The scenarios below demonstrate why the law was changed.

Table 4 shows how the spousal benefit of the same individual, Mary, would vary under three scenarios: (1) as a dually entitled recipient of Social Security retirement and spousal benefits; (2) as the recipient of a non-covered government pension and Social Security spousal benefits *before* the GPO was enacted; and (3) as the recipient of a non-covered government pension and Social Security spousal benefits *after* the GPO was enacted. In all three examples, it is assumed that Mary is potentially eligible for a Social Security spousal benefit of $1,000 per month, computed as 50% of her husband's monthly Social Security benefit of $2,000.

As a dually entitled retiree, under the first scenario, Mary's $1,000 Social Security spousal benefit is reduced by her own Social Security retired-worker benefit of $900, leaving her with a net spousal benefit of $100 and a total Social Security benefit of $1,000. Under the second scenario (where Mary receives a non-covered government pension instead of a Social Security retirement benefit), *before* the GPO takes effect, Mary's Social Security spousal benefits are not reduced at all and she receives a full Social Security spousal benefit of $1,000, plus the non-covered pension of $900, for total monthly pension benefits of $1,900. Under the third scenario (after the GPO was enacted in 1977), Mary's Social Security spousal benefit is reduced by two-thirds of her $900 non-covered government pension, leaving her with a net Social Security spousal benefit of $400 ($1,000 − $900*2/3) and a total monthly pension benefit of $1,300 ($900 from the non-covered pension + $400 from the Social Security spousal benefit).

Note that *the reduction to Social Security spousal benefits is smaller under the GPO than it is under the dual entitlement rule*: Mary receives monthly Social Security spousal benefits of $100 under the dual entitlement rule, compared with $400 under the GPO. Her total monthly retirement benefits are $1,000 under the dual entitlement rule, compared with $1,300 under the GPO. For those under dual entitlement, the Social Security spousal benefit is reduced by one dollar for every dollar of Social Security retirement benefits based on their own work histories in Social Security-covered employment. For those under the GPO, however, the Social Security spousal benefit is reduced by approximately 67 cents for every dollar of a pension from non-covered government employment.

Table 4. Mary's Spousal Benefit, Before and After GPO Enactment

	Mary works in Social Security-Covered Position	Mary works in Non-Social Security-Covered Position	
	Dually Entitled	Before GPO Enactment	After GPO Enactment
Social Security retired-worker monthly benefit (based on own earnings record)	$900	$0	$0
Non-Social Security-covered monthly pension	$0	$900	$900
Maximum Social Security spousal monthly benefit eligible to receive (based on spouse's earnings record), equal to 50% of the spouse's Social Security retirement benefit	$1,000	$1,000	$1,000
Reduction in spousal monthly benefit due to dual entitlement rule (equal to worker's Social Security retired-worker benefit)	$900	—	—
Reduction in Social Security spousal monthly benefit due to GPO (equals 2/3 of non-Social Security-covered pension)	—	—	$600
Actual Social Security spousal monthly benefit paid	$100	$1,000	$400
Total monthly retirement benefits paid to Mary (Social Security spousal benefit plus either (a) Social Security retired-worker benefit or (b) non-covered pension)	$1,000	$1,900	$1,300

Source: Illustrative example provided by CRS.

Notes: Dashes are used to represent scenarios in which either the dual entitlement rule or the GPO are not applicable. For example, in the dual entitlement scenario, Mary does not receive a non-covered government pension and, thus, the GPO does not apply.

Why a Two-Thirds Reduction?

The GPO was originally established in 1977 (P.L. 95-216) and replaced an earlier "dependency test" for spousal benefits that had been in law since 1950.[9] The 1977 law provided that 100% of the non-covered government pension be subtracted from the Social Security spousal or widow(er)'s benefit. If the original legislation had been left intact, the treatment of individuals affected by the dual entitlement rule and the GPO would have been identical because, in both cases, the Social Security spousal benefit would have been reduced by 100% of pension from non-covered employment.

The GPO's two-thirds offset to the non-government pension was established by the Social Security Amendments of 1983 (P.L. 98-21), which made a number of amendments to Social Security. One section of the House version of this law proposed that the amount used in calculating the offset be one-third of the government pension. The Senate version contained no such provision and would therefore have left standing the 100% offset that existed at the time. The conferees adopted the House bill except that the offset was fixed at two-thirds of the non-covered government pension.[10]

WHO IS AFFECTED BY THE GPO?

In 2009, the last year for which data are available, approximately 6.4 million state and local government workers (27.4% of all state and local government workers) were in non-Social Security-covered positions.[11] A government worker who does not pay into Social Security may potentially be affected by the GPO if he or she is entitled to a Social Security spousal benefit based on a spouse's or ex-spouse's work in Social Security-covered employment.

Generally, employees of the federal government hired before 1984 are covered by the Civil Service Retirement System (CSRS) and are not covered by Social Security; therefore, they may be subject to the GPO.[12] Most federal workers first hired into federal service after 1983 are covered by the Federal Employees' Retirement System (FERS), which includes Social Security coverage. Thus, although FERS retirees are not subject to the GPO, they, like all covered workers, may be subject to the Social Security dual entitlement rule.

As of December 2013, about 615,000 Social Security beneficiaries, or about 1% of all beneficiaries, had spousal or widow(er)'s benefits reduced by the GPO (not counting those who were potentially eligible for spousal or widow(er)'s benefits but were deterred from filing for them because of their expectation that the GPO would eliminate the spousal or widow(er)'s benefit). Of these persons subject to the GPO, 56% were spouses and 44% were widows and widowers. About 81% of all affected persons were women.[13] *Table 5* provides a breakdown of the affected beneficiaries by state and type of benefit.

Table 5. Number of Social Security Beneficiaries Affected by GPO, by State, Type of Benefit, and Offset Status, December 2013

State	Total	Spouses	Widow(er)s	Fully Offset Status[a]	Partially Offset Status[b]
Total	614,644	341,236	273,408	451,785	162,859
Alabama	4,365	1,915	2,450	3,383	982
Alaska	2,588	1,553	1,035	2,021	567
Arizona	7,985	4,299	3,686	6,142	1,843
Arkansas	2,965	1,506	1,459	2,311	654
California	91,550	55,138	36,412	76,870	14,680
Colorado	21,511	12,822	8,689	14,583	6,928
Connecticut	8,196	5,166	3,030	7,293	903
Delaware	561	246	315	442	119
District of Columbia	2,536	693	1,843	2,080	456
Florida	24,771	13,587	11,184	19,197	5,574
Georgia	16,866	8,660	8,206	12,554	4,312
Hawaii	1,948	1,019	929	1,606	342
Idaho	1,634	879	755	1,277	357
Illinois	43,723	25,858	17,865	36,931	6,792
Indiana	4,501	2,053	2,448	3,297	1,204
Iowa	1,851	871	980	1,381	470
Kansas	2,151	928	1,223	1,532	619
Kentucky	10,770	6,569	4,201	9,024	1,746
Louisiana	32,131	17,347	14,784	19,613	12,518
Maine	6,326	3,661	2,665	4,415	1,911
Maryland	9,185	3,218	5,967	7,289	1,896
Massachusetts	33,008	19,427	13,581	23,877	9,131
Michigan	5,672	2,756	2,916	4,316	1,356
Minnesota	5,872	3,142	2,730	4,849	1,023
Mississippi	2,855	1,332	1,523	2,190	665
Missouri	13,639	8,100	5,539	11,287	2,352
Montana	1,118	599	519	848	270
Nebraska	1,243	583	660	911	332
Nevada	8,547	4,878	3,669	6,720	1,827
New Hampshire	2,130	1,160	970	1,572	558
New Jersey	4,443	1,819	2,624	3,661	782
New Mexico	3,206	1,715	1,491	2,560	646

Table 5. (Continued)

State	Total	Spouses	Widow(er)s	Fully Offset Status[a]	Partially Offset Status[b]
New York	7,365	3,034	4,331	5,894	1,471
North Carolina	7,274	3,486	3,788	5,599	1,675
North Dakota	492	220	272	334	158
Ohio	86,019	49,230	36,789	52,325	33,694
Oklahoma	3,826	1,672	2,154	2,753	1,073
Oregon	4,351	2,332	2,019	3,287	1,064
Pennsylvania	7,906	3,295	4,611	6,040	1,866
Rhode Island	1,809	1,028	781	1,564	245
South Carolina	4,564	2,271	2,293	3,528	1,036
South Dakota	832	423	409	613	219
Tennessee	5,707	2,783	2,924	4,429	1,278
Texas	71,145	40,406	30,739	43,984	27,161
Utah	2,444	1,202	1,242	1,702	742
Vermont	630	340	290	479	151
Virginia	7,941	3,110	4,831	5,967	1,974
Washington	5,922	2,971	2,951	4,412	1,510
West Virginia	1,348	601	747	875	473
Wisconsin	3,411	1,775	1,636	2,715	696
Wyoming	533	275	258	385	148
Outlying areas and foreign countries	11,278	7,283	3,995	8,868	2,410

Source: Social Security Administration, Office of Research, Evaluation and Statistics, January 2014.

Notes: Includes persons entitled to spousal/widow(er)'s benefits only and those dually entitled to spousal/widow(er)'s and worker benefits.

[a] Individual received no Social Security spousal or widow(er)'s benefit because the reduction in the Social Security spousal benefit (a reduction equal to two-thirds of the pension from non-covered government employment) was greater than the Social Security benefit itself. Either the non-covered pension was large, or the potential Social Security benefit was small.

[b] Individual received partial Social Security spousal or widow(er)'s benefits because the reduction in the Social Security benefit (a reduction equal to two-thirds of the pension from non-covered government employment) was less than the Social Security benefit itself.

In December 2013, the average non-covered government pension amount for persons affected by the GPO was $2,188 per month ($1,977 for women and $3,063 for men).[14] The average pre-offset Social Security spousal benefit at that time was $753 per month ($821 for women and $468 for men).[15] The average reduction caused by the GPO was $613 per month ($650 a month for women and $460 for men).[16] The average Social Security spousal benefit component of the total benefit after application of the GPO was $140 per month ($172 a month for women and $9 a month for men).[17]

For approximately 74% of those with spousal or widow(er)'s benefits reduced by the GPO, the GPO reduction was large enough to fully offset any potential spousal or widow(er)'s benefit (because the non-covered pension was large and/or the potential Social Security spousal benefit was small).[18] Note that the total Social Security benefit received by a couple would be a larger amount, that is, the Social Security spousal benefit (after the GPO reduction) plus the primary worker's own Social Security benefit (which is not reduced by the GPO).

In comparison, in 2012, the dual entitlement rule affected approximately 6.8 million beneficiaries. About 6.7 million (97%) of all affected beneficiaries were women.[19] Wives made up 43% of all affected, and widows made up 54%. Among dually entitled workers, the average Social Security total benefit (retired worker plus spouse or survivor benefit) received was $1,128.[20] Of this amount, $633 was the retired worker component of the benefit. The spousal benefit component was $495 (after reduction for dual entitlement).[21] For the average dually entitled worker, therefore, the spousal benefit comprised about 44% of the total Social Security benefit received.

ISSUES

Opponents argue that the GPO is not well understood and that it harms lower-income workers. Defenders of the GPO maintain that it helps ensure that only financially dependent spouses receive the Social Security spousal benefit, while curtailing what otherwise would be an unfair advantage for government workers who are not covered by Social Security.

Awareness of the GPO and Retirement Preparedness

Critics of the GPO say that it is not well understood and that many affected by it are unprepared for a smaller Social Security benefit than they had assumed in making retirement plans. Supporters of the provision say it has been law for more than 35 years (it was enacted in 1977); therefore, people have had ample time to adjust their retirement plans. P.L. 108-203, passed in 2004, included a provision that sought to ensure that SSA and government employers notify potentially affected individuals about the effect of the GPO and the Windfall Elimination Provision (WEP).[22]

The SSA's personalized mailings to workers, entitled "Your Social Security Statement," contained a paragraph explaining the GPO and the WEP. Though SSA suspended the universal mailing of annual statements to in 2011 due to budget constraints, an online version that has retained the GPO and WEP educational material can be created for those who establish an online account.[23] So the material in the statements can continue to reach a broader audience, Congress directed SSA, in conjunction with the adoption of P.L. 113-76, the Consolidated Appropriations Act, 2014, to resume the mailing of statements to targeted groups and to those who are not able to successfully register for an online account.[24]

GPO Reduction Smaller than Dual Entitlement Reduction

The reduction to Social Security spousal benefits is smaller under the GPO than it is under the dual entitlement rule. Those under dual entitlement face a 100% offset to spousal benefits for every dollar received from a Social Security retired-worker benefit, whereas those under the GPO face an offset to spousal and widow(er)'s benefits equal to two-thirds of a non-Social Security-covered pension. In the example shown in *Table 4*, in which comparable spouses each receive a $900 retirement benefit based on their own work histories, the application of the 100% offset of the dual entitlement provision results in a $100 monthly Social Security spousal benefit for Mary. Comparatively, Mary qualifies for a $400 spousal benefit under the two-thirds offset of the GPO.

Parity Among Social Security-Covered Workers and Non-Covered Workers

The majority of state and local government workers, and federal employees hired since 1984, are covered by Social Security. Some argue that eliminating the GPO would be unfair to government employees in Social Security-covered positions, who would continue to be subject to the dual entitlement provision. As discussed above, for those under dual entitlement, the Social Security spousal benefit is reduced by one dollar for every dollar of Social Security retirement benefits based on their own work history in Social Security-covered employment. For those under the GPO, however, the Social Security spousal benefit is reduced by approximately 67 cents for every dollar of a pension from non-covered government employment.

Impact on Low-Income Workers

There is disagreement about the original intention of the GPO, which was enacted in 1977. Some argue that the original purpose was to prevent higher-paid workers from reaping over-generous spousal benefits. Others contest this, saying that the GPO was never targeted to a particular income group.

Opponents of the GPO argue that the provision hurts lower- and middle-income workers such as teachers and in some circumstances is sufficient to throw these workers into poverty. Opponents also say that the GPO is especially disadvantageous for surviving spouses.

An unpublished 2007 CRS analysis found that the common criticism that the GPO penalizes lower earners more than higher earners may not be accurate. The CRS analysis showed a great variation in outcomes.[25] In general, however, and holding other factors constant, the analysis found that low earners and some other individuals experience a much smaller offset to spousal benefits under the GPO than they would experience under the dual entitlement rule if the same work had been covered by Social Security. Others, including higher earners, experience a slightly larger offset to spousal benefits under the GPO than they would experience if the same work had been covered by Social Security and they had been subject to the dual entitlement rule.

Other evidence of the effect of the GPO on low earners comes from Social Security Administration data on the program. While 74% of those affected by the GPO have their benefits fully offset, about 27% of those with non-covered pensions of less than $1,000 per month had their benefits fully offset, compared with 75% of those with non-covered pensions between $1,001 and $1,999 and nearly 100% of individuals with non-covered pensions over that amount.[26] Among the group of individuals whose benefits were completely eliminated by the GPO, less than 10% of this group had a non-covered pension amount of less than $1,000 per month.[27] Thus, if the non-covered pension amount is a reflection of the approximate earnings levels of individuals affected by the GPO, a greater percentage of those with lower earnings receive at least a partial Social Security benefit relative to the overall GPO-affected population.

Regarding concerns about pushing those affected by the GPO into poverty, in 2001 the poverty rate among those affected by the GPO was approximately 6.0%, whereas the poverty rate for those affected by the dual entitlement rule was approximately 8.9%.[28] The poverty rate for all Social Security beneficiaries aged 65 and older was about 8.5%. For comparison purposes, the poverty rate for the general population at that time was approximately 11.3%.

Imprecision of the Two-Thirds Offset to Non-Covered Government Pensions

Opponents point out that whatever the rationale for the GPO, reducing everyone's spousal or widow(er)'s benefit by two-thirds of their government pension is an imprecise way to estimate what the spousal benefit would have been if the government job had been covered by Social Security. If two-thirds of the government pension were in fact a good proxy for Social Security retirement benefits, there would be no significant difference in outcomes between the dual entitlement rule and the GPO. As noted above (see the previous section, "Impact on Low-Income Workers"), however, there is great variation in outcomes. The GPO may lead to a smaller offset relative to the dual entitlement rule for low earners than for high earners.

Ideally, opponents argue, the way to compute the offset to replicate the dual entitlement rule would be to apply the Social Security benefit formula to a spouse's total earnings, including the non-covered portion, and reduce the resulting Social Security spousal benefit by the proportion of total earnings attributable to non-covered earnings. Currently, however, the SSA does not have complete records of non-covered earnings histories. Although SSA started collecting W-2s in the early 1980s, the initial records were sometimes incomplete. The Social Security benefit formula requires earnings data for a worker's entire lifetime.

Application of the GPO to Government versus Private Pensions

Some question why the GPO does not apply to the spousal benefits received by the spouses of private sector workers, who may receive private, employer-sponsored pensions (defined benefit or defined contribution) in addition to Social Security benefits. Generally, the private sector employment on which the private pension is based would be covered by Social Security. Therefore, the dual entitlement rule (which the GPO is meant to replicate) would instead take effect to reduce any Social Security spousal benefits for which a beneficiary might be eligible. As noted earlier, in many cases the dual entitlement rule would produce a higher reduction in spousal benefits than does the GPO.

Cost of Eliminating the GPO

Some argue that weakening or eliminating the GPO would be costly at a time when neither Social Security nor the federal budget is in sound financial condition. In 2007, SSA projected the 10- year cost of repealing the GPO to be about $42 billion.[29] Such a move could also lead to demands for repeal of the dual entitlement rule to ensure parallel treatment for those working in Social Security-covered employment. In 2003, SSA estimated that eliminating the dual entitlement rule would cost approximately $500 billion over a five-year period.[30]

THE GPO "LAST-DAY" RULE

A burgeoning controversy arose in the 108th Congress with the revelation that a growing number of state and local government workers had been making use of a little-known provision of the law that allowed them to escape the application of the GPO if they switched jobs at the very end of their government careers. That provision granted an exception to the GPO if, on the last day of one's government service, he or she worked in a Social Security-covered position. On August 15, 2002, the Government Accountability Office (GAO) released a report that found that, as of June 2002, 4,819 individuals in Texas and Georgia had switched to Social Security-covered positions to avoid the application of the GPO to their Social Security spousal benefits. The GAO projected that the cost to the program for these cases could be about $450 million.[31]

On February 11, 2004, the House of Representatives agreed to Senate amendments and passed H.R. 743, the Social Security Protection Act of

2003, which became P.L. 108-203.[32] As discussed below, P.L. 108-203 eliminated the last-day exception clause by requiring those workers switching from non-covered positions to Social Security-covered positions to work in the covered position for at least 60 months (five years) before being exempt from the GPO.[33] The new GPO provision became effective for Social Security spousal benefit applications filed after March 31, 2004.

How Does the Last-Day Rule Affect Exemption from the GPO?

Any current Social Security beneficiary who is receiving spousal benefits and is exempt from the GPO because they retired from their non-covered position in government under the last-day rule would continue to be exempt from the GPO. Individuals may still be exempt from the GPO if

- *They applied for Social Security spousal benefits before April 1, 2004, and work their last day in a Social Security-covered position within the same retirement system.* In this case, an individual who received a Social Security spousal benefit before April 1, 2004, could continue to work in a non-covered position and still make use of the last-day rule when he retires from government employment, regardless of when the retirement occurs.

- *Their last day of government service occurred before July 1, 2004, and they worked their last day in a Social Security-covered position within the same retirement system.* In other words, if a worker switched from non-covered government work to Social Security-covered work for her last day of work within the same retirement system, she is exempt from the GPO, even if she files for Social Security benefits at a later date. However, if a worker returns to work in a non-covered position in the same retirement system that she previously retired from and new contributions are made by either the employee or employer to the non-covered pension system, her last-day exemption from the GPO will be revoked and she will be subject to the new 60-month requirement for exemption from the GPO.

- *Their last day of government service occurs on or after July 1, 2004, and before March 2, 2009, and they work a total of 60 months in a Social Security-covered position within the same retirement system.* The required 60-month period of Social Security-covered employment would be reduced by the number of months the worker performed in Social Security-covered employment under the same retirement system prior to March 2, 2004. However, in no case can the 60-month requirement be reduced to less than one month. For example, a teacher who is currently working in a non-covered position but who previously worked for 12 months in a Social Security-covered position under the same retirement system would have the 60-month requirement reduced to 48 months. The remaining months to be worked (in this case 48 months), must be worked consecutively and after March 2, 2004. Thus, if he switched to a covered position in the same retirement system as his prior government work for at least the final 48-month period of his employment and his last day of employment was before March 2, 2009, he would be exempt from the GPO.

- *Their last day of government service occurs after March 3, 2009, and they work their last 60 months in a Social Security-covered position within the same retirement system.*

All other individuals receiving government pensions based on non-covered employment would be subject to reductions in Social Security spousal benefits under the GPO.

End Notes

[1] The GPO is often confused with the Windfall Elimination Provision (WEP), which reduces Social Security benefits that a person receives as a worker if he or she also has a government pension based on work that was not covered by Social Security. For additional information in the Windfall Elimination Provision (WEP), please refer to CRS Report 98-35, Social Security: The Windfall Elimination Provision (WEP), by Gary Sidor.

[2] Social Security Administration, Social Security Basic Facts, January 14, 2014, available at http://www.ssa.gov/ legislation/2014factsheet.pdf.

[3] Social Security Administration, unpublished table, "Estimated Social Security Coverage of Workers with State and Local Government Employment, 2009" (the most recent year for which data are available).

[4] Ibid. The disparity in coverage among states occurs because, while Social Security originally did not cover any state and local government workers, over time the law has changed. Most state and local government employees became covered by Social Security through voluntary agreements between the Social Security Administration (SSA) and individual states, known as "Section 218 Agreements" because they are authorized by §218 of the Social Security Act. Beginning in July 1991, state and local employees who were not

members of a public retirement system or covered by a Section 218 agreement were mandatorily covered by Social Security.

[5] The dual entitlement rule requires that 100% of a Social Security retirement or disability benefit earned as a worker (based on one's own Social Security-covered earnings) be subtracted from any Social Security spousal benefit one is eligible to receive (based on a spouse's Social Security-covered earnings). So, in cases where the spousal benefit is higher than the worker's own benefit, the worker receives his or her own worker benefit plus the reduced spousal benefit, which is the difference between the spousal benefit and the worker's own benefit. In cases where the worker's own benefit is higher than the spousal benefit, the worker receives only his or her own benefit.

[6] Social Security Administration, Annual Statistical Supplement 2013, Washington, DC, 2014, Table 5.G2, http://www.ssa.gov/policy/docs/statcomps/supplement/2013/5g.pdf and Table 5.A1, http://www.ssa.gov/policy/docs/ statcomps/supplement/2013/5a.pdf.

[7] Social Security Administration, Office of Research Evaluation and Statistics, unpublished Table A, January 2014.

[8] In this example, John is not eligible for a Social Security spousal benefit because Mary's employment was not covered by Social Security.

[9] The dual entitlement rule has been in law since 1939, when spousal benefits were introduced.

[10] Effectively, the GPO offset formula assumes that two-thirds of the government pension is roughly equivalent to the Social Security retirement (or disability) benefit the spouse would have earned as a worker if his or her job had been covered by Social Security.

[11] Social Security Administration, unpublished table, "Estimated Social Security Coverage of Workers with State and Local Government Employment in 2009."

[12] Workers who switch from CSRS to FERS must work for five years under FERS in order to be exempt from the GPO.

[13] Social Security Administration, Office of Research Evaluation and Statistics, unpublished Table DE01, January 2014.

[14] Ibid., Table G209, January 2014; data are limited to those beneficiaries for whom the offset amount is available.

[15] Ibid., Table G309, January 2014; data are limited to those beneficiaries for whom the offset amount is available. Includes persons entitled to spousal/widow(er)'s benefits only and those dually entitled to spousal/widow(er)'s and worker benefits. For a dually entitled beneficiary, the pre-offset Social Security benefit is the difference between the larger spousal/widow(er)'s benefit and the smaller worker benefit.

[16] Ibid., Table G609, January 2014; data are limited to those beneficiaries for whom the offset amount is available.

[17] Ibid., Table G509, January 2014; data are limited to those beneficiaries for whom the offset amount is available. Amounts may not add due to rounding.

[18] Ibid., Table G105, January 2014; data are limited to those beneficiaries for whom the offset amount is available.

[19] Social Security Administration, Annual Statistical Supplement, 2013, Table 5.G2, available at http://www.ssa.gov/ policy/docs/statcomps/supplement/2013/5g.pdf. The term "dually entitled" applies only to those who receive spousal benefits. If an individual's own worker benefit is greater than his or her spousal benefit, that person receives the higher worker benefit and is not considered "dually entitled." Administrative data do not provide the number of people in this latter category.

[20] Ibid., Table 5.G3.

[21] Ibid.

[22] The WEP reduces Social Security benefits that a person receives as a worker if he or she also has a government pension based on work that was not covered by Social Security.

[23] Social Security Administration at http://www.ssa.gov/myaccount/.

[24] Social Security Administration plan to increase the number of individuals receiving Social Security Statements, March 2014, http://www.ssa.gov/legislation/Social%20Security%20Statement%20Plan.pdf.

[25] How an individual would be affected by the GPO versus the dual entitlement rule is determined by several key variables, including the relative earnings level of the individual, the timing of the worker's non-covered employment during his or her career, and the number of years in non-covered employment. The primary difference between outcomes among high- and low-earners is driven by the fact that a worker's Social Security benefit (the basis for the dual entitlement offset, which reduces the spousal benefit by 100% of this amount) is progressive, while pensions from non-covered government employment (the basis for the GPO reduction, which reduces spousal benefits by two-thirds of this amount) generally provide a pension that is the same fixed percentage of earnings regardless of the earnings level. As earnings rise, if the earnings are from non-covered employment then the pension from this employment rises proportionately; if the earnings are from covered employment, then the Social Security benefit, which is progressive, rises less than proportionately. Hence for high earners, the GPO offset to spousal benefits, which is two-thirds of non-covered pensions and which rises proportionately as income rises, becomes more significant than the dual-entitlement offset to spousal benefits, which involves a 100% offset to the Social Security benefit and which rises more slowly as income rises. In general, any combination of variables (such as earnings level, timing of non-covered employment, or number of years in non-covered employment) that increases the size of the non-covered government pension more than it increases the size of the Social Security benefit (assuming the same earnings were covered by Social Security) would make the dual entitlement rule more advantageous to an individual than the GPO.

[26] CRS calculations based on data provided by the Social Security Administration's Office of Research, Evaluation and Statistics, unpublished Table I, January 2014.

[27] Ibid.

[28] Poverty rates were calculated by David Weaver of the Social Security Administration's Office of Retirement Policy using the March 2001 Current Population Survey (CPS). Poverty status is taken directly from the CPS and is thus subject to errors in the reporting of income. The sample for the GPO and dually entitled poverty rates only includes persons for whom SSA administrative records could be matched. The sample size for the GPO poverty rate is relatively small (130 cases). The poverty rates for the Social Security beneficiary population age 65 and over and for the general population do not require matched data and are based completely on CPS data. Updated data for this comparison are not available.

[29] Social Security Administration, Memorandum from Bert M. Kestenbaum and Tim Zayatz of the Office of the Chief Actuary, "Estimated Additional OASDI Benefit Payments Resulting From Several Proposals to Modify the Windfall Elimination Provision and the Government Pension Offset—INFORMATION," October 26, 2007. SSA has not published a more recent estimate.

[30] Social Security Administration, Memorandum from Bert Kestenbaum of the Office of the Chief Actuary, "Estimated Additional OASDI Benefit Payments from Proposals to Eliminate or Change the Dual-Entitlement Offset Provision— INFORMATION," April 17, 2003. SSA has not published a more recent estimate.

[31] Government Accountability Office, Report GAO-02-950, Revision to the Government Pension Offset Exemption Should Be Reconsidered, August 15, 2002.

[32] For more information on H.R. 743, see SSA's legislative bulletin on P.L. 108-203, http://www.socialsecurity.gov/ legislation/legis_bulletin_030404.html.

[33] This five-year period for GPO exemption is consistent with that required of federal employees converting from CSRS to FERS.

INDEX

Index 123

U

U.S. Department of Labor, 14, 43, 44, 45
U.S. Social Security Administration, 10, 11, 44
United, 43, 44, 45, 49, 57, 90
United States, 43, 44, 45, 49, 57, 90
urban, 44
Urban Institute, 44, 45, 46, 47

V

variables, 117
Vice President, 48
volatility, 21, 31

W

wage level, 35, 89
wages, viii, 2, 18, 27, 31, 47, 56, 58, 72, 83, 88, 95

Washington, 9, 10, 11, 13, 14, 15, 16, 43, 44, 45, 46, 47, 48, 49, 82, 84, 90, 92, 95, 108, 116
well-being, 15
WEP, v, x, 37, 50, 87, 88, 89, 90, 91, 93, 94, 95, 110, 115, 117
widowers, vii, 1, 5, 46, 107
widows, vii, 1, 11, 15, 17, 18, 23, 24, 26, 31, 74, 107, 109
windfall elimination provision, x, 37, 50, 87, 88, 89, 93
Wisconsin, 92, 108
work effort, vii, x, 26, 54, 55, 72
work records, vii, viii, x, 2, 10, 12, 15, 28, 31, 54, 97, 99
worker benefits, x, 3, 11, 14, 15, 49, 62, 97, 99, 108, 116
workforce, vii, viii, 1, 2, 4, 28, 29, 31, 72, 73
working mothers, 29